Quick and Easy
KNITS

Quick and Easy
KNITS

100 Little Knitting Projects
to Make

Search Press

First published in 2019

Search Press Limited
Wellwood, North Farm Road,
Tunbridge Wells, Kent TN2 3DR

Previously published in 2016 as *100 Little Knitted Gifts to Make*
using material from the following books in the *Twenty to Make*
series published by Search Press:

Knitted Cakes by Susan Penny, 2008
Knitted Mug Hugs by Val Pierce, 2010
Knitted Bears by Val Pierce, 2010
Knitted Aliens by Fiona McDonald, 2010
Knitted Flowers by Susie Johns, 2010
Mini Christmas Knits by Sue Stratford, 2011
Knitted Fruit by Susie Johns, 2011
Knitted Baby Bootees by Val Pierce, 2011
Knitted Vegetables by Susie Johns, 2011
Knitted Beanies by Susie Johns, 2012
Knitted Boot Cuffs by Monica Russel, 2012
Easy Knitted Scarves by Monica Russel, 2013
Knitted Phone Sox by Susan Cordes, 2013
Knitted Wrist Warmers by Monica Russel, 2014
Easy Knitted Tea Cosies by Lee Ann Garrett, 2014
Knitted Headbands by Monica Russel, 2015

Text copyright © Susan Penny, Val Pierce, Fiona McDonald,
Susie Johns, Sue Stratford, Monica Russel, Susan Cordes,
Lee Ann Garrett 2016

Photographs by Roddy Paine, Debbie Patterson, Paul Bricknell,
Vanessa Davies, Fiona Murray, Laura Forrester

Photographs and design copyright
© Search Press Ltd 2016

ISBN: 978-1-78221-802-9

Suppliers
If you have difficulty in obtaining any of the materials and
equipment mentioned in this book, then please visit the Search
Press website for details of suppliers: www.searchpress.com

CONTENTS

Abi Ballet Bear, page 40

Pearly Phone Sock, page 44

Celtic Braid Mug Hug, page 46

Coffee Cupcake, page 48

Fragmolite Alien, page 50

Peas in a Pod, page 52

Strawberry, page 54

Lacy Fern Headband, page 56

Little Cable Cuffs, page 58

Steely Tweed Scarf, page 60

Panda Beanie, page 62

Simply Blue Bootees, page 66

Imperium Boot Cuffs, page 68

*Grapes Tea Cosy,
page 70*

*Gingerbread Heart,
page 72*

Cactus Flower, page 74

*Barney College Bear,
page 76*

*Black Cat Phone Sock,
page 78*

*Cottage Garden
Mug Hug, page 80*

Fruit Tart, page 82

Pilquat Alien, page 84

Sweetcorn, page 86

Pineapple, page 88

*Flossie Headband,
page 90*

*Lilac Wrist Warmers,
page 92*

*Parisienne Chic Scarf,
page 94*

*Rolled-up Beanie,
page 96*

*Bumblebee Boots,
page 98*

*Hemingway Boot Cuffs,
page 100*

*Nautical Tea Cosy,
page 102*

*Mini Christmas Stocking,
page 104*

*Grape Hyacinth,
page 106*

*Olivia Sweetheart Bear,
page 108*

*Funky Orange
Phone Sock, page 112*

*Coffee and Cream
Mug Hug, page 114*

Jazzy Cake, page 116

*Grosperneatt Alien,
page 118*

Pumpkin, page 120

*Bunch of Grapes,
page 122*

*Gooseberry Headband,
page 124*

*Scallop Wrist Warmers,
page 126*

*Pompom Scarf,
page 128*

*Long, Cool Beanie,
page 130*

*Candy Pink Bootees,
page 132*

*Penguin Boot Cuffs,
page 134*

*Ladybug Tea Cosy,
page 136*

Mini Rudolph, page 138

Tulip, page 142

*Emily Knitting Bear,
page 144*

*Sideways Phone Sock,
page 148*

*Lady's Smock Mug Hug,
page 150*

Angel Cake, page 152

Jorna Alien, page 154

Mushroom, page 156

Cherries, page 158

Red Robin Headband, page 160

Frosty Wrist Warmers, page 162

Autumn Haze Scarf, page 164

Flower Power Beanie, page 166

Duckling Bootees, page 168

Love My Boot Cuffs, page 170

Strawberry Tea Cosy, page 172

Mini Snowman, page 174

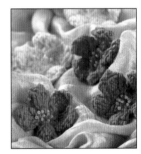

Cherry Blossom, page 178

Poppy Panda Bear, page 180

*Curious Sheep
Phone Sock, page 182*

*Warm and Woolly
Mug Hug, page 184*

*Cupcake Egg Cosy,
page 188*

Verna Alien, page 190

Asparagus, page 192

Blackberry, page 194

*Two-tone Cable
Headband, page 196*

Sparkler Cuffs, page 198

*Zebra Razzle Scarf,
page 200*

*Knit Knit Beanie,
page 202*

*Rosie Toes Bootees,
page 204*

*Blueberry Bouclé
Boot Cuffs, page 206*

*Valentine's Day Tea Cosy,
page 208*

What a Hoot, page 210

Arum Lily, page 214

Ellie Bouquet Bear, page 216

Wise Owl Phone Sock, page 218

Strawberry Fair Mug Hug, page 220

Iced Doughnut, page 222

Carrot, page 224

Plum, page 226

Chic Stripey Cuffs, page 228

Classic Beanie, page 230

Pumpkin Tea Cosy, page 234

Nordic Bunting, page 236

Daisy, page 238

INTRODUCTION

If you love knitting, *Quick and Easy Knits* is the perfect book for you. With 100 quick and easy patterns to choose from, there are lots of projects that will appeal to competent beginners and more advanced knitters alike. Designed by eight talented and experienced authors, these fabulous projects are the work of Sue Stratford, Val Pierce, Susie Johns, Monica Russel, Lee Ann Garrett, Susan Cordes, Susan Penny and Fiona McDonald.

The range of projects includes knitted beanies, flowers, scarves, boot cuffs, phone sox, tea cosies, teddy bears, baby bootees, fruit and vegetables, cupcakes, aliens, headbands, wrist warmers and mini Christmas knits, so there is something here for everyone to choose from. There is a useful section on knitting know-how and useful techniques at the beginning, which explains what you need to make these charming projects. Every single one of these beautiful knitted items will make lovely, personalised gifts for family and friends.

Projects include a Celtic Braid mug hug, an Owl tea cosy, Pompom baby bootees, a Lacy Fern headband, a Heather & Skye scarf, Lilac wrist warmers, Olivia Sweetheart Bear, a Classic Beanie, a Curious Sheep phone sock, a Daisy, Blueberry Bouclé boot cuffs and Nordic Bunting. The techniques used are suitable for knitters of all skill levels and include cables, lace and intarsia as well as stockinette (stocking) stitch and garter stitch.

Whatever the occasion, there is a wealth of inspiration here with projects that will make the perfect gift for birthdays, christenings, anniversaries, weddings, Valentine's Day, Halloween and Christmas.

Happy knitting!

KNITTING KNOW-HOW

Yarn

Most yarn today comes in hanks or skeins. These are big loops of yarn that are bought by weight and thickness. Before knitting they need to be wound into a ball so that the yarn does not get knotted. Some yarns can be bought ready-prepared as balls. These come in different weights and thicknesses and you can knit directly from them.

There are a variety of yarns used in the projects in this book and these can be substituted for those of your choice. It is advisable to check the length and weight of yarn that you buy against the ones used in the patterns to ensure that you have enough to finish your projects.

Lace yarn (1–3 ply) is a very fine yarn that is used for more open patterns. Generally, you get very long yardage in a 50g ball or hank. Sometimes lighter weight yarns can be doubled to create a more dense look.

Light worsted (DK/8-ply) yarn is a medium thickness yarn that is very versatile and suitable for many projects. This is the most popular weight of yarn.

Worsted (aran/10-ply) yarn is thicker than light worsted (DK/8-ply) yarn and will produce knitted items that are thicker than those made with other weights.

Bulky (chunky) and super bulky (super chunky) weights of yarn are thicker, work up more quickly than lighter weights of yarn and are ideal for bulkier projects.

Knitting needles

Needles are available in metal, plastic and wood. Those made from sustainable wood are very comfortable to work with, extremely durable and flexible to work with in all temperatures.

For some of the projects you will need cable needles or circular needles. Many people find that the yarns stay on needles made from sustainable wood better than metal or plastic needles. Experiment to find out what suits you best.

Gauge (tension)

Some projects, such as garments or other items that need to be a particular size (such as tea cosies), will require you to work to a specific gauge (tension). Details of this are included with the pattern. It is a good idea in such cases to knit a gauge (tension) swatch to the manufacturer's guidelines of 4 x 4in (10 x 10cm) in stockinette stitch (UK stocking stitch); these swatches will also be helpful if you decide to use alternative yarns to those used in the projects.

Other items

For all of the projects you will need a pair of good-quality, sharp scissors to cut off the ends of yarns when sewing them into your work.

As well as knitting needles, you will also need a blunt-ended needle with a large eye, such as a tapestry needle, for sewing up all your projects and weaving in any loose ends. You may also need a crochet hook, a sewing needle and embroidery thread for some projects.

Abbreviations

Many common knitting abbreviations used in this book are listed in the table below.

alt:	alternate	rep:	repeat
cm:	centimetres	RS:	right side
dec:	decrease	skpo:	slip 1, knit 1, pass slipped stitch over
DPN:	double-pointed needles		
foll:	following	sl:	slip a stitch
GS:	garter stitch (knit every row)	SM:	slip marker from left to right needle
in	inches		
inc:	increase (by working into the front and back of the stitch)	SS:	stockinette stitch (UK stocking stitch) – alternate knit and purl rows
K:	knit		
Kfb:	knit into the front and back of the stitch (increasing one stitch)	ssk:	slip 2 sts knitwise one at a time, pass the two slipped sts back to left needle, knit both together through the back of the loop
K2tog:	knit 2 stitches together		
M:	marker		
M1:	make a backwards loop on your needle by twisting the yarn towards you and slipping the resulting loop on to the right-hand needle. On the following row knit or purl through the back of the st.	ssp:	slip 2 sts knitwise one at a time, pass two slipped sts back to left needle, purl two slipped sts together from the back, left to right
		st(s):	stitch(es)
P:	purl	tbl:	through the back of the loop
PM:	place marker	tog:	together
P2tog:	purl 2 stitches together	W&T:	wrap and turn (see page 19)
psso:	pass slipped stitch over	WS:	wrong side
rem:	remaining	YO:	yarn over needle, resulting in another stitch

USEFUL TECHNIQUES

There are a number of knitting techniques that come in very handy for things such as joining your pieces together and making up your projects. Those below are the most frequently used in this book.

Making up

Many of the projects are sewn together using a darning or tapestry needle and the same yarn the item has been knitted in. If any other needles (for example, a sewing needle) are required, they are listed with the individual patterns.

Mattress stitch

Mattress stitch makes a practically invisible and nicely flexible seam for joining pieces together.

1 With the right sides of the work facing, start with your yarn in the lower right corner. Take your tapestry needle across to the left edge and under the strand of yarn between the first and second stitches of the first row.

2 Take your needle back to the right edge and insert it one row up, between the first and second stitches of the row.

3 Take your needle back to the left edge and repeat stages one and two.

4 After completing a few stitches, gently pull the long end of the yarn to draw the stitches together.

This stitch will make your seam virtually invisible.

Cable cast-on

This technique is used in patterns where you need to cast on in the middle of a row.

Insert your knitting needle between the first two stitches, wrap the yarn around your needle and bring it through to the front of your work. Transfer the newly created stitch onto the left-hand needle, thus increasing a stitch.

Casting on using the finger or thumb method

1 Make a slip knot leaving a long tail. Put the slip knot on the knitting needle; hold the knitting needle in your

right hand and use the tail to make a loop on your index finger (or thumb) of your left hand (this finger or thumb becomes the other knitting needle).

2 Insert the needle into the loop on your finger or thumb and knit the stitch.

3 Continue in this manner until you have the required number of stitches on your knitting needle.

I-cord

I-cords are very useful when you need to make long, thin pieces of knitting, such as Rudolph's antlers (see page 138), or the Snowman's arms (see below). To make an i-cord, cast on your stitches using a double-pointed needle, knit them and slide them to the other end of the same needle, then pull the yarn across the back of the needle and knit the stitches again. Repeat these instructions until the cord is long enough. By pulling the yarn behind the stitches on the needle, you close the 'gap' and give the appearance of French knitting. Alternatively, you can work the stitches in stocking stitch and sew up the seam.

I-cord arms
The Snowman's arms are made using i-cords (see page 174).

Wrap and turn

This technique ensures you do not end up with a 'hole' in your knitting when working short row shaping and turning your work mid row. Slip the following stitch from the left needle to the right needle. Move the yarn from the back to the front of the work, between the needles, and slip the stitch back to the left-hand needle. Turn the work.

Moss stitch

This simple but effective stitch gives a really interesting, deep texture to your knitted fabric and looks a lot more complicated than it is.

Row 1: (K1, P1) to end of row.

Row 2: (P1, K1) to end of row.

Therefore, on the second row you are purling the stitches you have knitted on Row 1 and knitting the stitches you have purled on Row 1.

French knots

French knots are a simple way of providing surface decoration which is very attractive. You can use them to make flowers (see Cottage Garden mug hug on page 80), eyes (see the Snowman opposite), or simple bobble shapes (see the Coffee Cupcake below). Bring the needle up from the back of the work through to the front and

French knot decoration
The Coffee Cupcake is decorated with simple bobble shapes (see page 48).

wind the yarn around the needle twice. Take the needle through the work, half a stitch away, holding the loops around the needle with your finger while pulling the yarn through to the back of your work. Fasten off.

Blanket stitch

Thread a darning needle with yarn and bring to the front of your work about $3/8$in (1cm) from the edge. Leaving a small gap along the edge of the work, take the needle to the back of the work approximately $3/8$in (1cm) in from the edge and bring it back to the front at the edge of the knitting. Loop your yarn under the needle and pull it through until it lays neatly against the emerging yarn. Repeat this process.

Running stitch

This is a simple embroidery stitch that is very useful for surface decoration. Thread your sewing needle and begin by bringing your thread up from the underside of the material or knitted work, then taking the needle back down, leaving a space from the beginning of your work. Continue in this manner, making sure that the spaces between your stitches are even.

Making pompoms

Pompoms are great embellishments to things such as bootees (see page 30), hats (see page 202) or scarves (see page 128). To make a pompom, cut two circles of cardboard, each $2 3/8$in (6cm) in diameter and cut a 1in (2.5cm) diameter hole in the centre of each. Thread a tapestry needle with four 2yd (2m) strands of yarn. Hold the two cardboard discs together and pass the needle through the holes, over the outside edges and back though the centre again.

Continue wrapping the ring in this way until the whole ring is covered with an even layer of yarn. Using sharp scissors, cut through the yarn around the edges of the circles, inserting the tips of the blades between the two cardboard circles. Cut two $11 3/4$in (30cm) lengths of the same yarn and insert the two strands between the cardboard layers and around the cut yarn, pulling tightly and knotting firmly to hold the bundle of short strands in place.

Remove the card discs and fluff out the pompoms, then cut off any stray ends and trim to the desired size.

*This textured headband is made from
a super soft yarn in a subtle colour.
The flower gives it a vintage look.*

DUSTY HEADBAND

Materials:
1 ball of worsted (aran/10-ply) baby alpaca/merino yarn in dusky pink; 50g/103yd/94m
1 button (optional)

Needles:
1 pair of 5mm (UK 6, US 8) and 1 pair of 4mm (UK 8, US 6) knitting needles

Instructions:

Using size 5mm (UK 6, US 8) knitting needles, cast on 17 sts.

Little flakes stitch

This is worked on an uneven number of stitches.

Row 1: Purl.

Row 2: Knit.

Row 3: *make 3 sts from 1 st (knit, purl, knit all into the same st), p1, rep from * to last st, work 3 sts into the last st.

Row 4: p3, *k1, p3, rep from * to end.

Row 5: k3, *p1, k3, rep from * to end.

Row 6: As row 4.

Row 7: k3tog, *p1, k3tog, rep from * to end.

Row 8: p1, *k1, p1, rep from * to end.

Row 9: p1, *knit, purl, knit all into the same st, p1, rep from * to end.

Row 10: k1, *p3, k1, rep from * to end.

Row 11: p1, *k3, p1, rep from * to end.

Row 12: As row 10.

Row 13: p1, *k3tog, p1, rep from * to end.

Row 14: k1, *p1, k1, rep from * to end.

Repeat rows 3–14 until work is long enough to fit around your head when slightly stretched.

Making up

With RS together, join the end seams using mattress stitch.

6-petal flower (optional)

Using 4mm (UK 8, US 6) needles, cast on 4 sts.

**Row 1 and every wrong side row: Purl.

Row 2 (RS): *k1, inc1, rep from * to last st, k1 (7 sts).

Row 4: *k1, inc1, rep from * to last st, k1 (13 sts).

Row 6: Knit.

Row 8: k5, sk2po, k5 (11 sts).

Row 10: k4, sk2po, k4 (9 sts).

Row 12: k3, sk2po, k3 (7 sts).

Row 13: Purl.

Cut yarn leaving a reasonable length and leave the 7 sts on the needle.

On the second needle, cast on 4 sts and rep from ** five more times (six petals in total), leaving RS facing for the next row (42 sts in total on needle).

Continue as follows:

Row 14 (RS): k6, k2tog, *k5, k2tog, rep from * three more times, k6 (37 sts).

Row 15: *p2tog, rep from * to last st, p1 (19 sts).

Row 16: Knit.

Row 17: *p2tog, rep from * to last st, p1 (10 sts).

Row 18: *k2tog, rep from * to end (5 sts).

Row 19: Pass second, third, fourth and fifth sts over the first stitch.

Cut yarn, and pass through remaining st.

Making up

Pull up ends at the base of each petal and then using each end in turn, sew adjacent petals together to approximately ½in (1.5cm) from the base. Sew in all ends of yarn by weaving them into the back of the work. Sew the button onto the centre of the flower and then sew the flower onto the headband. Attach the tips of the top and bottom petals to the headband to prevent the flower flopping over.

BLAZE
WRIST WARMERS

Instructions:

Both cuffs are identical. Using 5.5mm (UK 5, US 9) needles, cast on 28 sts.

Rows 1–6: *k1, p1* repeat from * to * to end of row.

Rows 7–8: k1, *yo, k2tog*, rep from * to * to last st, k1.

Rows 9–10: Knit.

Rows 11–12: st st.

Rows 13–14: Knit.

Rows 15–16: st st.

Repeat rows 7–16 until work measures 7in (18cm), ending with a row 16.

Next row: k2tog *p1, k1*, rep from * to * to last 2 sts, p2tog.

Next two rows: *k1, p1*, rep from * to * to end of row.

Next row: Cast off all sts.

Making up

Using a tapestry needle and mattress stitch, join the seam 2¾in (7cm) from the finger end (cast-off) edge and 3½in (9cm) from the wrist end (cast-on) edge. This will leave a gap for your thumb to go through.

Weave in all loose ends.

Materials:

1 ball of worsted (aran/10-ply) yarn, variegated with a red base; 100g/142yd/130m

Needles:

1 pair of 5.5mm (UK 5, US 9) knitting needles

23

These wrist warmers are simple to knit and the texture and colour of the yarn make them stand out from the crowd.

HEATHER & SKYE SCARF

Materials:

- 1 ball of super bulky (super chunky) yarn in green/purple variegated; 250g/240yd/220m
- 1 large wooden button
- Purple darning yarn

Needles:

- 1 pair of 12mm (UK 000; US 17) knitting needles

Knitting note

This was made using a handspun and dyed yarn from a cottage industry in Skye, Scotland. I simply knitted the scarf until the yarn ran out. The amount listed is therefore an estimate. Using an easily available bouclé super bulky (super chunky) yarn of approximately 250g and 240½yd (200m) will make a good substitute.

Instructions:

Using 12mm (UK 000, US 17) needles, cast on 9sts in green/purple variegated yarn.

Scarf pattern

Row 1: k1, *wyrn, k2tog* repeat from * to *.

Next rows: Repeat row 1 until work measures 39in (1m).

Cast off sts.

In this pattern there are significant gaps between some stitches. Instead of making a specific buttonhole, one of these can be used when fastening the button.

Identify such a hole, then, in a position in which it can be fastened comfortably, sew on a button using purple darning yarn and a tapestry needle.

Making up

Using a large-eyed needle, sew in the ends of the yarn by weaving them into the rear of the scarf.

This scarf was inspired by a visit to Skye. I really loved the colours of the heathers and ferns and so bought handspun and locally dyed wool in colours to match them.

BLOSSOM BEANIE

Materials:
2 balls of light worsted (DK/8-ply) acrylic yarn in ivory; 50g/148yd/135m

Large button 1⅜in (3.5cm)

Needles:
3.75mm (UK 9, US 5) knitting needles

Size:
To fit an average female adult head

Gauge (tension)
22 sts and 30 rows to 4in (10cm) measured over stocking stitch.

Vintage Petals
The past continues to have an influence on today's fashions and this hat, in a style that flatters most face shapes, evokes the classic elegance of a bygone era. The pull-on cloche – the French word for 'bell' – became the must-have fashion accessory in the 1920s: a head-hugging style designed to be worn low on the forehead. Embellished with a five-petalled flower, this version has a wide horizontal band and slightly slouchy styling, which makes it comfortable to wear.

Instructions:

Ribbed band
Cast on 22 sts.

Row 1: sl1, (k2, p2) five times, k1.

Rep row 1 167 times; cast off in pattern; do not cut yarn but pick up and knit 78 sts along long edge (including st already on needle).

Crown
Row 1: inc1 in each st (156 sts).

Row 2: purl.

Row 3: (k12, inc1) twelve times (168 sts).

Beg with a p row, work 22 rows in stocking stitch.

Row 26: (k12, k2tog) twelve times (156 sts).

Row 27 and each odd-numbered (WS) row: purl.

Row 28: (k11, k2tog) twelve times (144 sts).

Row 30: (k10, k2tog) twelve times (132 sts).

Row 32: (k9, k2tog) twelve times (120 sts).

Row 34: (k8, k2tog) twelve times (108 sts).

Row 36: (k7, k2tog) twelve times (96 sts).

Row 38: (k6, k2tog) twelve times (84 sts).

Row 40: (k5, k2tog) twelve times (72 sts).

Row 42: (k4, k2tog) twelve times (60 sts).

Row 44: (k3, k2tog) twelve times (48 sts).

Row 46: (k2, k2tog) twelve times (36 sts).

Row 48: (k1, k2tog) twelve times (24 sts).

Row 49: (p2tog) twelve times (12 sts).

Row 50: (k2tog) six times.

Cut yarn, leaving a long tail, and thread through rem 6 sts.

Flower petals (make 5)
Cast on 5 sts.

Row 1: inc in each st to end (10 sts).

Row 2: purl.

Row 3: inc in each st to end (20 sts).

Row 4: purl.

Row 5: inc in each st to end (40 sts).

Beg with a purl row, work 3 rows in stocking stitch.

Cast off; cut yarn and fasten off.

Centre
Cast on 5 sts.

Row 1: inc in each st to end (10 sts).

Row 2: purl.

Row 3: inc in each st to end (20 sts).

Beg with a purl row, work 3 rows in stocking stitch.

Cut yarn and thread through all sts.

Making up
Stitch the cast-on and cast-off rows of the ribbed band together using a running stitch, then pull up to gather and fasten off. With right sides facing, join the seam on to the crown with mattress stitch.

Join the straight edges of each petal using a running stitch, then pull up very slightly to flatten the centre of the petal. Stitch the five petals in place, overlapping, across the gathered join on the ribbed band. Join the seam on the flower centre, then run a gathering stitch around the edge of the circle.

Place a large button on the wrong side and pull up the tail of yarn to gather around the button, then stitch the flower centre firmly in place in the middle of the five petals.

POMPOM BOOTEES

Instructions:

Make two.

Cast on 29 sts using the thumb method (see page 18).

Rows 1–4: GS.

Row 5: (RS facing) P2, *K1, P2*, rep from * to * to end.

Row 6: K2, *P1, K2*, rep from * to * to end.

Rows 7–28: rep rows 5 and 6 eleven times.

Row 29: knit.

Row 30: purl.

Divide for instep as follows:

Row 31: K9, (P2, K1) three times, P2, turn and slip rem 9 sts on to a stitch holder.

Row 32: K2, (P1, K2) three times, slip rem 9 sts on to second stitch holder.

Row 33: (P2, K1) three times, P2.

Row 34: K2, (P1, K2) three times.

Rows 35–50: working on these 11 sts, rep rows 33 and 34 eight times.

Break yarn.

Slip 9 sts from second holder on to the free needle with point at inner end, rejoin yarn and pick up and knit 11 sts along first side of instep. Knit across 11 sts on needle, pick up and knit 11 sts down other side of instep then knit across 9 sts from first stitch holder (51 sts).

Work in GS on these sts for 11 rows.

Shape foot as follows:

Next row: K2tog, K17, K2tog, K9, K2tog, K17, K2tog.

Next row: knit.

Next row: K2tog, K15, K2tog, K9, K2tog, K15, K2tog.

Next row: knit.

Cast off.

Making up
Work in the ends carefully. Join the leg and underfoot seams neatly. Fold over the top of each bootee to form a cuff. Make two small pompoms (see page 19). Trim them to a neat shape and sew one to the front of each bootee.

These boot cuffs will give a
different look to a favourite
pair of boots. Try knitting them
in cream yarn for a classic
monochrome look.

BRAMBLE BOOT CUFFS

Materials:

3 balls of super bulky (super chunky) yarn in purple; 100g/87½yd/80m

Tools:

1 pair of 7mm (UK 2, US 10½) DPN, 7.5in (19cm)

1 x 10mm (UK 000, US 15) circular needle, 23½in (60cm)

1 stitch marker

Instructions:

Cuffs (make 2)

Using 7mm DPN and purple yarn, cast on 29 sts, distributing the stitches evenly across four of the needles.

Do not turn work. Join this first round by slipping the first cast-on stitch on to the left-hand needle. PM on right-hand needle (this is to mark the beginning of the round), and knit this slipped stitch together with the last cast-on stitch. You will now have 28sts (7 on each of the DPNs).

Rows 1–16: *k1, p 1* rep to the end of the row. These 16 rows form the cuff of the piece. Be careful to move your stitch marker at the end of each row.

Legs

Continuing from the cuffs, change to the 10mm (UK 000; US 15) circular needle and begin bramble stitch as follows. The pattern repeat is over four stitches. Remember to PM after each completed round.

Round 1: p.

Round 2: *p1, k1, p1* all into next st, k3 together, rep set pattern to the end of the round.

Round 3: p.

Round 4: k3tog, *p1, k1, p1*, rep set pattern to the end of the round.

These four rounds create the bramble stitch. Rep the four rounds one more time and then rep row 1 once more. Cast off sts purlwise.

Weave in all loose ends.

Feathered friend
Using a white-flecked brown yarn gives a lovely rustic look to the cosy, but don't be afraid to experiment with bright or bold shades to create a more colourful character!

OWL TEA COSY

Materials:

1 ball of worsted (aran/10-ply) yarn in brown, plus oddments in cream, yellow and black; 100g/213yd/195m

Two black buttons

Needles:

1 pair of 4mm (UK 8, US 6) knitting needles and 1 pair of 4.5mm (UK 7, US 7) DPN

Gauge (tension)

5 sts = 1in (2.5cm).

Instructions:

Using brown yarn and 4mm (UK 8, US 6) needles, cast on 42 sts.

Knit in SS until work measures 16½in (42cm) from the cast-on edge.

Making up

Fold the wrong sides of the cosy together (right sides facing out).

Sew the top

Thread a tapestry needle with one of the brown tails at the top of the cosy. Sew down one side for approximately 2½in (6.5cm). Fasten off, hide tail in seam. Repeat on other side of cosy.

Sew the bottom

Thread a tapestry needle with one of the brown tails of yarn from the cast on edge. Sew up one side for approximately 1½in (4cm). Fasten off, hide tail in seam. Repeat on the other side of cosy.

Eye (make 2)

Using cream yarn and the 4.5mm (UK 7, US 7) DPN, cast on 6 sts.

Row 1: knit.

Row 2: kfb in each st.

Rows 3–16: knit.

Row 17: k2tog across row.

Cast off those 6 sts.

Eye centre

Using yellow yarn and the 4.5mm (UK 7, US 7) DPN, cast on 3 sts.

Row 1: kfb in each st.

Row 2: kfb in each st.

Row 3: *k1, kfb*, repeat from * to * to end of row.

Row 4: knit.

Cast off.

Shape into a circle and sew seam.

Pupils

Sew a black button to the middle of the centre eye.

Beak

Using black yarn and the 4.5mm (UK 7, US 7) DPN, cast on 2 sts.

Row 1: knit.

Row 2: purl.

Row 3: kfb, kfb.

Row 4: purl.

Row 5: knit.

Row 6: purl.

Row 7: kfb, k2, kfb.

Row 8: purl.

Row 9: knit.

Row 10: purl.

Row 11: kfb, k4, kfb.

Row 12: purl.

Row 13: knit.

Row 14: purl.

Row 15: k2tog across row.

Cast off purlwise.

Ear tufts (make 2)

Take a piece of cardboard about 3in (8cm) wide and wrap black yarn around it about ten times. Slide the yarn loop off the cardboard and, with another piece of black yarn, tie a knot around the loop about ¾in (2cm) from one end. Wind the yarn tightly up to the top then down around this ¾in (2cm). Secure the thread, then sew the tufts on to the points of the tea cosy and trim the ends.

TWINKLING STAR

Instructions:

Star points (make 5)

Holding a strand of gold yarn and a strand of sequin yarn together, cast on 2 sts and K 2 rows.

Next row: K1, M1, K1 (3 sts).

K 2 rows.

Next row: K1, K1fb, K1 (4 sts).

K 1 row.

Next row: K2, M1, K2 (5 sts).

K 1 row.

Next row: K2, K1fb, K2 (6 sts).

Place sts of each point on a spare needle or stitch holder.

Centre of star

With RS facing, K across all five points of the star (30 sts).

Next row: (K1, K2tog) to end of row (20 sts).

K1 row.

Next row: K2tog to end of row (10 sts).

K1 row.

Thread yarn through rem sts and draw up, fasten off and sew side seam of star.

Make a second star shape in the same way.

Making up

With WS together, sew the stars carefully together, folding all the loose ends into the inside of the star and stuffing gently with toy filling as you go.

Materials:

Small amount of fingering (4-ply) yarn in gold

Small amount of sequin yarn

Toy filling

Tools:

1 pair 3.25mm (UK 10, US 3) knitting needles

Spare needle or stitch holder

Size:

Approx. 3⅛in (8cm) from point to point

37

Starry Night

Make other stars in silver and you have a starry firmament of Christmas decorations for the tree or around the house.

The deep pink water lily could make a big, bold corsage to wear on a winter coat or a felt hat or beret. To knit the pale pink alternative, make up the flower using a textured pale pink yarn and make the flower centre with an acid yellow mohair yarn for a textural contrast.

WATER LILY

Materials:

Small amounts of light worsted (DK/8-ply) yarn
  in bright pink and bright yellow

Needles:

1 pair of 3mm (UK 11, US 2) knitting needles

Size:

Approx. 4¾in (12cm) across

39

Instructions:

Outer flower

Cast on 9 sts.

Row 1: k all sts tbl.

Row 2: k.

Row 3: inc 1, k to end (10 sts).

Row 4: k.

Row 5: inc 1, k to end (11 sts).

Row 6: k.

Row 7: inc 1, k to end (12 sts).

Row 8: k.

Row 9: k2tog, k to end (11 sts).

Row 10: k.

Row 11: k2tog, k to end (10 sts).

Row 12: k.

Row 13: k2tog, k to end (9 sts).

Row 14: k.

Row 15: cast off 6, k to end.

Row 16: k3, cast on 6 (8 sts).

Rep rows 1–16 three times more
and rows 1–14 once, then cast off
all sts; break yarn and fasten off.

Inner flower

Cast on 8 sts.

Row 1: k all sts tbl.

Row 2: k.

Row 3: inc 1, k to end (9 sts).

Row 4: k.

Row 5: inc 1, k to end (10 sts).

Next 3 rows: k.

Row 9: k2tog, k to end (9 sts).

Row 10: k.

Row 11: k2tog, k to end (8 sts).

Row 12: k.

Row 13: cast off 5, k to end.

Row 14: k3, cast on 5 (8 sts).

Rep rows 1–14 twice more and
rows 1–12 once, then cast off all
sts; break yarn and fasten off.

Centre

Cast on 6 sts.

Row 1: cast off 5 sts, turn.

Row 2: cast on 5 sts.

Rep rows 1 and 2 seven times more,
then cast off all sts; break yarn and
fasten off.

Making up

Join the two ends of the outer
flower by stitching the lower
corners of the two end petals
together, then run a thread along
the base of all the petals and pull
up tightly to gather; do the same
with the inner flower and the flower
centre. Stitch the inner flower on
top of the outer flower, matching
centres. Stitch the
flower centre in place.

ABI BALLET BEAR

Materials:

1 ball each of light worsted (DK/8-ply) yarn in beige
   and pale pink; 50g/137yd/125m

Small quantity of toy stuffing

2 x 6mm round black beads for eyes

Black embroidery thread or floss for features

Sewing needle

Pink net for under skirt, 4 x 15¾in (10 x 40cm)

1 pink satin ribbon, pearl and rose embellishment

4 small ribbon roses

19¾in (50cm) sparkly pink ribbon edging

Strong thread for sewing

39½in (1m) pink double-sided satin ribbon,
   ¼in (5mm) wide

Tools:

1 pair 3.25mm (UK 10, US 3) knitting needles

Sewing needle

Stitch holder

Instructions

Work the bear entirely in GS, unless otherwise stated.

Bear's head

Cast on 30 sts.

Rows 1–4: GS.

Row 5: K2, skpo, knit to last 3 sts, K2tog, K1.

Rows 6–7: GS.

Continue to dec in this way on every third row until 8 sts rem.

Next row: K2, skpo, K2tog, K2.

Next row: K2, skpo, K2.

Next row: K1, sl1, K2tog, psso, K1.

Next row: K3tog.

Fasten off.

Body and legs (make 2 pieces the same)

Cast on 12 sts.

Rows 1–2: GS.

Rows 3–8: inc 1 st at each end of rows 3, 5 and 7 (18 sts).

Rows 8–33: knit.

Row 34: divide for legs. K8, cast-off 2, knit to end (8 sts).

Proceed on these 8 sts for first leg.

Rows 35–52: knit.

Row 53: K2tog, knit to last 2 sts, K2tog.

Row 54: cast off.

Return to stitches left on needle, rejoin yarn and complete to match first leg.

Arms (make 2)

Cast on 6 sts.

Row 1: knit.

Row 2: knit twice into each st to end (12 sts).

Rows 3–6: knit.

Row 7: inc 1 st at each end of row (14 sts).

Rows 8–27: knit.

Rows 28–30: dec 1 st at each end of rows 28 and 30 (10 sts).

Row 31: K2, (K2tog) three times, K2 (7 sts).

Row 32: knit.

Cast off (this is the top of the arm).

Making up

Make up the head by folding the three corners of the triangle into the centre; the fold lines are shown in the top diagram opposite. Sew the two side seams either side of the nose, and across the corner lines to form the ears, as shown in the lower diagram.

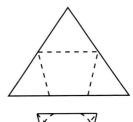

Sew a little way along the neck seam, just down from the nose. Stuff the head firmly to give it a good shape. Stitch on the nose and mouth with black thread, and sew on the eyes.

Stitch the back and front body pieces together using a flat seam on the right side of the work. Leave the neck edge open for stuffing. Stuff firmly and then close the neck opening. Attach the head to the body.

Shoes (make 2)

Using an appropriate colour and 3.25mm (UK 10; US 3) needles, cast on 14 sts.

Next row: knit.

Next row: inc in each st across row (28 sts).

Work 5 rows GS.

Next row: K2tog, K8, (K2tog) four times, K8, K2tog.

Next row: K9, (K2tog) twice, K9.

Next row: knit.

Cast off. Stitch the seam along the base and back of the shoe. Put a tiny amount of stuffing inside the shoe, place the base of the leg inside the shoe and stitch it in place. Add embellishments.

Dress (bodice front)

Using pink yarn, cast on 24 sts.

Rows 1–6: SS.

Rows 7–8: cast off 2 sts at beg of each row.

Rows 9–10: SS.

Row 11: dec 1 st at each end of row (18 sts).

Row 12: purl.

Rows 13–16: SS.

Divide for neck

Work 7 sts, slip next 4 sts on to stitch holder, work 7 sts.

Continue on first 7 sts for side of neck.

Dec 1 st at neck edge on next and following alt rows until 4 sts rem.

Cast off.

Work other side to match.

Bodice back

Work rows 1–16 of bodice front.

Rows 17–21: SS.

Cast off.

Skirt

With RS facing, pick up and knit 24 sts along cast-on edge of bodice front.

Next row: purl.

Next row: knit twice into each st (48 sts).

Continue in SS until skirt measures 5cm (2in). Work 2 rows in GS.

Repeat the above, on bodice back.

Cast off.

Neckband

Join one shoulder seam.

With RS facing, pick up and knit 5 sts down one side of neck, 4 sts from stitch holder across front of neck, 5 sts up other side of neck and 10 sts around back of neck (rem 4 sts will form other shoulder).

Next row: knit.

Cast off knitwise.

Making up the dress

Stitch one shoulder seam and work the neckband. Sew the side seams, turn right-side out and slip the dress on to the bear. Catch together the neckband and shoulder seam. Tie a length of ribbon around the waist and tie in a bow at the back. Attach the ribbon, pearl and rose embellishment to the front of the dress at the waistline. Stitch the pink edging around the hem and neckline.

Ballet slippers (make 2)

Using pink yarn, cast on 14 sts, and work in SS.

Next row: knit.

Next row: inc in each st across row (28 sts).

Work 5 rows in SS.

Next row: P2tog, P8, (P2tog) four times, P8, P2tog.

Next row: K9, (K2tog) twice, K9.

Next row: purl.

Cast off. Stitch the seam along the base and back of the shoe. Put a tiny amount of stuffing inside the shoe, place the base of the leg inside the shoe and stitch it in place.

Take a short length of pink ribbon, approximately 8cm (3¼in) long, and stitch one end to the right-hand side of the left-hand slipper at the front. Take it across the front of the shoe to the left, and wrap it around the back of the bear's leg. Bring it back round to the front and catch it in place on the left-hand side of the slipper. Sew a ribbon rose to the centre front. Finish the other slipper to match.

Finishing off

Take the net and fold it in half lengthwise. Gather the folded edge (this is the top) until it fits around the bear's waist. Slip it on to the bear and secure. Sew the side seam. Catch it in place under the skirt of the dress. Make a small bow with pink ribbon and stitch two ribbon roses to the centre of it. Place the decoration on the bear's head and stitch it in place, using the photograph as a guide.

PEARLY PHONE SOCK

Materials:

- 1 ball of light worsted (DK/8-ply) yarn in cream; 50g/131yd/120m
- Toggle clasp, button or large hook and eye
- 11 x small pearl beads
- Cream embroidery thread

Tools:

- 1 pair of 4mm (UK 8, US 6) knitting needles
- 3.75mm (UK 8/9, US F) crochet hook
- Sewing needle
- Scissors
- Tape measure

Knitting note

You may find it easier to stitch the pearls on to the phone sock before you close the side seams – just make sure you attach them to the right side.

Instructions:

Using 4mm (UK 8, US 6) needles, cast on 28 sts in cream using the finger or thumb method (see page 18).

Row 1: k4, p4 to end.

Row 2: p4, k4 to end.

Row 3: k4, p4 to end.

Row 4: p4, k4 to end.

Row 5: p4, k4 to end.

Row 6: k4, p4 to end.

Row 7: p4, k4 to end.

Row 8: k4, p4 to end.

Next rows: Rep rows 1–8 pattern until work measures 4in (10cm).

Cast off 14 stitches (keep pattern).

Continue working on the remaining stitches, keeping to the pattern for 1¼in (3cm).

Cast off loosely, then leave the last stitch on your needle to use as the first stitch for the crochet.

Making up

Transfer the final stitch on to your crochet hook and work the attached chain stitch method around the flap and opening, making a loop of 6 detached chain for the loop.

Close the side seams with mattress stitch, then attach the button using a needle and thread. Weave in any loose ends.

Add pearl beads in the recessed squares (see opposite), attaching them with needle and thread.

Perfect for cosy nights in front of the fire, these chunky mug hugs will keep your drink hot.

CELTIC BRAID MUG HUG

Materials:

1 ball of light worsted (DK/8-ply) yarn in leaf-
green; 50g/137yd/125m

1 green flower button

Needles:

1 pair of 4mm (UK 8, US 6) and 1 pair of 3.25mm
(UK 10, US 3) knitting needles

1 cable needle

Size:

Approx. 9¾ x 2¼in (25 x 6cm)

Abbreviations

CB3: slip next 3 sts on to cable needle and leave at
back of work. Knit next 3 sts, then knit 3 sts from
cable needle.

CF3: slip next 3 sts on to cable needle and leave at
front of work. Knit next 3 sts, then knit 3 sts from
cable needle.

Instructions:

Using 4mm (UK 8, US 6) needles
and green yarn, cast on 26 sts.

Commence cable pattern as
follows:

Row 1: K1, P3, K18, P3, K1.

Row 2: K4, P18, K4.

Row 3: K1, P3, (CB3) three times,
P3, K1.

Row 4: K4, P18, K4.

Row 5: K1, P3, K18, P3, K1.

Row 6: K4, P18, K4.

Row 7: K1, P3, K3, (CF3) twice, K3,
P3, K1.

Row 8: K4, P18, K4.

Continue in pattern until work
measures 9in (23cm) ending on
either row 3 or row 7.

Change to 3.25mm (UK 10; US 3)

needles and dec 7 sts evenly across
row (19 sts).

Working in GS, dec 1 st at each end
of next and every alt row until 9 sts
rem. Cast off.

Using 3.25mm (UK 10, US 3)
needles, pick up and knit 19 sts
along the other short edge.

Knit 1 row.

Continue in GS.

Dec 1 st at each end of next and
every alt row until 13 sts rem.

Next row: to make buttonhole,
K2tog, K4, yrn twice, K2tog, K3,
K2tog.

Next row: knit, dropping the yrn of
the previous row and knitting into
the loops.

Continue to dec as before until
9 sts rem.

Cast off.

Making up

Weave in all loose ends. Attach the
green flower button to correspond
to the buttonhole at the other end.

The mocha cup cake is stitched in chocolate-coloured wool and decorated with dark wooden beads.

COFFEE CUPCAKE

Materials:

1 ball each of light worsted (DK/8-ply)
  pure merino yarn in cream and coffee;
  50g/57yd/53m

1 ball of fingering (4-ply) 100% cotton yarn
  in white; 50g/169yd/155m

A pearl bead

A 2¼in (60mm) polystyrene craft ball
Toy stuffing

Needles:

1 pair of 4mm (UK 8, US 6), 1 pair of 2.25mm
  (UK 13, US 1) and 1 pair of 3.25mm (UK 10,
  US 3) knitting needles

Instructions:

Top of cake

Cast on 40 sts in cream yarn using 4mm (UK 8, US 6) knitting needles.

Rows 1–4: st st for 4 rows.

Rows 5–10: change to coffee and g st for 6 rows.

Row 11: (K4, K2tog) to last 4 sts, K4 (34 sts).

Row 12: knit.

Row 13: knit, decreasing 6 sts randomly across row (28 sts).

Row 14: knit.

Row 15: knit, decreasing 4 sts randomly across row (24 sts).

Row 16: knit.

Break yarn, leaving a long end. Thread through stitches on needle and draw up tightly.

Side of case

Cast on 60 sts using white cotton fingering (4-ply) yarn and 2.25mm (UK 13, US 1) needles.

Rows 1–11: K1, P1 across row for 11 rows.

Row 12: inc every second P st across row.

Cast off.

Base of case

Cast on 10 sts using white cotton fingering (4-ply) yarn and 2.25mm (UK 13, US 1) needles. Work in st st.

Row 1: * purl.

Row 2: knit, increasing 1 st at beg and end of row. *

Rows 3–8: repeat rows 1 and 2 from * to * (18 sts).

Rows 9–11: continue in st st.

Rows 12–18: dec 1 st at beg and end of every K row (10 sts).

Row 19: purl.

Cast off.

Flower

Using 3.25mm (UK 10, US 3) needles and cream yarn, follow the instruction for a single swirl of piped cream on page 6. Break yarn and thread it through the single stitch on the needle. Repeat for each petal.

Making up

Join the side seam of the cup cake case, then stitch the bottom in place. Join the side seam of the cup cake top. Pull up the thread holding the stitches at the top of the cake, and darn the thread end in to hold it firmly in place. Attach the petals to the top of the cake, adding a bead to the centre. Using cream wool, make French knots on the top of the cake. Position the cake top inside the cup cake case. Insert a polystyrene craft ball, adding some stuffing to pad out the shape, then catch-stitch the top to the bottom.

These cute little water-loving aliens have a fluffy 'skirt' worked in multicoloured yarn to complete their look.

FRAGMOLITE ALIEN

Materials:

1 ball each of light worsted (DK/8-ply)
    yarn in turquoise, yellow and brown;
    50g/137yd/125m

Small amount of multicoloured fluffy yarn

2 beads for eyes

Toy stuffing

Sewing thread

Needles:

1 pair of 3mm (UK 11, US 2) knitting needles

Sewing needle

Instructions:

Body (make 1)

Cast on 20 sts in turquoise.
Rows 1–5: st st.
Rows 6–10: Change to fluffy yarn. Continue in g st.
Rows 11–18: Change to yellow yarn.
Continue in st st and cast off.

Head (make 1)

Using turquoise yarn, cast on 3 sts.
Row 1: inc in each st (6 sts).
Row 2: purl.
Row 3: inc in each st (12 sts).j
Row 4: purl.
Row 5: inc each st (24 sts).
Rows 6–16: st st.
Row 17: *k3, inc 1* rep from * to * to end (30 sts).
Rows 18–20: st st.
Row 21: k6.
Rows 22–32: Turn and work on 6 st only in st st.
Row 33: k2tog each end (4 sts).
Row 34: purl.
Row 35: k2tog twice and cast off.
Repeat this pattern on each of the 4 sets of 6 stitches to get 5 tentacles in all.

Arms (make 2)

Cast on 3 sts in brown.
Row 1: inc each st (6 sts).
Rows 2–16: st st.
Row 17: k2tog each end (4 sts).
Row 18: purl.
Row 19: k2tog twice and cast off.

Legs (make 2)

Cast on 3 sts using yellow.
Row 1: inc each st (6 sts).
Rows 2–6: st st.
Rows 7–8: Change colour on knit row to brown and knit 1 row. Purl one row in same colour. Rows 9–10: Change colour on knit row to yellow and knit 1 row. Purl one row in same colour.
Rows 11–18: Swap colour on next knit row and repeat sequence until you have 3 contrasting stripes (excluding the foot).
Rows 19–24: st st. Cast off on last purl row.

Making up

Fold body in half and secure the centre back seam and bottom seam with mattress stitch (make sure side seam is back seam). Stuff with toy stuffing and sew the top shut. Fold each tentacle in half and mattress stitch along the length of the tentacle. Sew the centre back head seam up. Run thread around the opening under the head and gather it together. Stitch the head to body. Mattress stitch along the arm and leg seams. The limbs do not need to be stuffed. Attach the legs at the base of the body and the arms at the shoulders.

PEAS IN A POD

Instructions:

Peas (make 4)
With set of four 3mm (UK 11, US 2) DPN and light green yarn, cast on 6 sts and distribute these equally between three needles.

Round 1: inc1 in each st (12 sts).

Round 2–25: k.

Round 26: (k2tog) six times (6 sts).

Break yarn and thread through rem sts.

Pod (make 1)
With 3mm (UK 11, US 2) needles and bright green yarn, cast on 24 sts.

Row 1: k22, turn.

Row 2: k20, turn.

Row 3: k18, turn

Row 4: k16, turn.

Row 5: k14, turn.

Row 6: k12, turn.

Row 7: k10, turn.

Row 8: k8, turn.

Row 9: k6, turn.

Row 10: k4, turn.

Row 11: k2, turn.

Row 12: k to end; cast off, leaving last st on needle.

Pick up and knit 24 sts along opposite edge of cast-on row.

Rep rows 1–12.

Do not break yarn.

Stalk (make 1)
Cast on 11 sts (12 sts).

Next row: cast off.

Materials:
- 1 ball each of light worsted (DK/8-ply) wool, acrylic or blended yarn in light green and bright green; 50g approx. 137yd/125m
- 4 x wooden beads

Needles:
- Set of four 3mm (UK 11, US 2) DPN and 1 pair of 3mm (UK 11, US 2) knitting needles

Making up
For the peas, insert four wooden beads into the tube of knitting and use spare yarn to bind tightly between each one. Next, place the row of peas inside the pod and oversew a few stitches at either end. The finished pea pod measures approximately 1in (2.5cm) wide and 3½in (9cm) long, excluding the stalk.

Strawberries and Dreams
Make a whole punnetful of strawberries, with or without stalks, as a celebration of summer.

STRAWBERRY

Materials:
1 ball of light worsted (DK/8-ply) wool or acrylic yarn in red and a small amount in green; 50g/137yd/125m

Toy stuffing

Needles:
1 pair of 3.25mm (UK 10, US 3) and 1 pair of 3mm (UK 11, US 2) knitting needles

Instructions:

Strawberry
With size 3.25mm (UK 10, US 3) needles and red yarn, cast on 6 sts.

Row 1: (inc1, k1) three times (9sts).

Row 2: p.

Row 3: (inc1, k2) three times (12 sts).

Row 4: p.

Row 5: (inc1, k3) three times (15 sts).

Row 6: p.

Row 7: (inc1, k4) three times (18 sts).

Row 8: p.

Row 9: (inc1, k2) six times (24 sts).

Row 10: p.

Row 11: (inc1, k3) six times (30 sts).

Row 12: p.

Row 13: k.

Row 14: p.

Row 15: (k2tog, k3) six times (24 sts).

Row 16: (k2tog) twelve times (12 sts).

Row 17: (k2tog) six times (6 sts).

Row 18: (k2tog) three times (3 sts).

Cast off.

Calyx and stalk
*With 3mm (UK 11, US 2) needles and green yarn, cast on 1 st.

Row 1: (RS) k.

Row 2: inc2 (3 sts).

Row 3: k1, p1, k1.

Row 4: k.

Row 5: k1, p1, k1.

Row 6: k1, inc2 in next st, k1 (5 sts).

Row 7: k1, p3, k1.

Row 8: k.

Row 9: k1, p3, k1; cut yarn and transfer sts to a stitch holder or spare needle.*

Rep from * to * three times more.

With right side of work facing, k across all sts on spare needle (20 sts).

Row 10: (p2tog) ten times (10 sts).

Cut yarn and thread through the first 8 sts, leaving 2 sts on needle for stalk.

Row 11: k2; do not turn but slide sts to other end of needle.

Rows 12–15: Rep row 11 four times more; then fasten off.

Making up
Graft the edges of the strawberry together, stuffing it with toy stuffing as you go. On the calyx, turn under the edges on each point, using the yarn ends to secure, then stitch it to the top of the strawberry.

LACY FERN HEADBAND

Materials:

1 ball of lace weight (2-ply) alpaca/silk yarn
in fern green; 100g/800m/875yd

Needles:

1 pair of 3mm (UK 11, US 2) knitting needles

Instructions:

The lace pattern is knitted in multiples of 8 + 5.

Cast on 37 sts.

Row 1 (RS): Knit.

Row 2: Purl.

Row 3: k1, p3, *k5, p3, rep from * to last st, k1.

Row 4: p1, k3, *p5, k3, rep from * to last st, p1.

Row 5: k1, yfrn, k3tog, yfrn, *k5, yfrn, k3tog, yfrn, rep from * to last st, k1.

Rows 6–8: Stocking stitch starting with a purl row.

Row 9: k5, *p3, k5, rep from * to end.

Row 10: p5, *k3, p5, rep from * to end.

Row 11: k5, *yfrn, k3tog, yfrn, k5, rep from * to end.

Row 12: Purl.

Repeat these 12 rows until the headband fits snugly around your head with a slight stretch, ending with either a row 6 or a row 12.

Cast off all sts.

Making up

With RS of work together, join seams together using mattress stitch. Weave in all loose ends.

Twist it, fold it or wear it flat – this headband is very versatile. The lacy stitch gives the band movement, so you can create your own look.

These useful cuffs will keep your hands warm on a winter's day, whether cycling, walking or working on a computer, as they allow you to have totally free hands. I have chosen a classic colour for this design and a gorgeous alpaca yarn, but they could equally well be knitted in a bright colour.

LITTLE CABLE CUFFS

Materials:

2 balls of light worsted (DK/8-ply) yarn in fawn;
50g/131yd/120m

Needles:

1 pair of 4mm (UK 8, US 6) and 1 pair of 4.5mm
(UK 7, US 7) knitting needles

1 cable needle

Knitting note

Cr3F: slip next 2 sts onto a cable needle and hold
at front of work, p1, then k2 from cable needle.

Cr3B: slip next st onto cable needle and hold at
back of work, k2, then p1 from cable needle.

C4B: Place 2 sts on to a cable needle and place
at back of work. Knit next 2 sts, then knit 2 sts
from the cable needle.

C4F: Place 2 sts on to a cable needle and place
at front of work. Knit next 2 sts, then knit 2 sts
from the cable needle.

Instructions:

The pattern is the same for both hands, and the yarn is
used double throughout.

Using 4mm (UK 8, US 6) needles cast on 37 sts, then
ktbl to form a neat edge.

Row 1: *k1, p1*, rep from * to * to last st, k1.

Row 2: *p1, k1*, rep from * to * to last st, p1.

Rows 3–16: As rows 1 and 2, except inc 1 st at the start
and inc 1 st at the end of row 16 (39 sts).

Change to 4.5mm (UK 7, US 7) needles for the following
cable section of the pattern.

Rows 1, 3, 9 and 11: (WS) *p2, k2, p2, k1, p2, k2, p2*,
rep from * to * twice more.

Row 2: *k2, p2, slip next 3 sts onto cable needle and
hold at back of work, k2, slip the purl st from cable
needle back onto left-hand needle and purl it, k2 from
cable needle, p2, k2*, rep from * to *
twice more.

Rows 4 and 12: *Cr3F, Cr3B, p1, Cr3F, Cr3B*, rep from *
to * twice more.

Rows 5, 7, 13 and 15: *k1, p4, k3, p4, k1*, rep from * to
* twice more.

Rows 6 and 14: *p1, C4B, p3, C4F, p1*, rep from * to *
twice more.

Rows 8 and 16: *Cr3B, Cr3F, p1, Cr3B, Cr3F*, rep from *
to * twice more.

Row 10: *k2, p2, slip next 3 sts onto cable needle and
hold at front of work, k2, slip the purl st from cable
needle back onto left-hand needle and purl it, k2 from
cable needle, p2, k2*, rep from * to *
twice more.

Change to 4mm (UK 8, US 6) needles.

Row 17: *k2, p2*, rep from * to * to last 3 sts,
k2, p1.

Cast off all sts.

Making up

With RS facing, use a tapestry needle and mattress
stitch to join the side seams.

Weave in all loose ends.

STEELY TWEED SCARF

Instructions:

Throughout the pattern, knit one strand of A and one strand of B
together to produce the tweed effect.

Initial rows

Rows 1–2: Using 5mm (UK 6, US 8) needles cast on 45 sts, ktbl on
return row (i.e. row 2).

Scarf pattern

Rows 1 and 3: p3, *k1, sl1, k1, p3*, repeat from * to * to end
of row.

Rows 2 and 4: *k3, p1, k1, p1*, repeat from * to * to last 3 sts, k3.

Rows 5 and 7: k4, *sl1, k5*, repeat from * to * to last 4 sts, k4.

Rows 6 and 8: p4, *k1, p5*, repeat from * to * to last 4 sts, p4.

Next rows: Continue knitting rows 1–8 until scarf measures 66½in
(169cm). Cast off sts. Sew in loose sts by weaving them into the
knitting at the rear of work.

Making tassels

Wind black wool around the short sides of the CD case and cut it in
the centre to make lengths for the tassels.

Use four strands at a time and a 5mm (UK 6, US 8/H) crochet
hook to thread the wool through the scarf to make 17 tassels for
each end.

*A classic look that is
knitted by using shades
of alpaca wool together.
Black tassels add interest.*

PANDA BEANIE

Materials:

- 2 balls of worsted (aran/10-ply) wool and cashmere blend yarn in cream; 50g/98yd/90m
- 1 ball of light worsted (DK/8-ply) 100% wool yarn in black; 50g/137yd/125m
- 2 x sew-on googly eyes

Needles and tools:

1 pair of 4mm (UK 8, US 6) and 1 pair of 5mm (UK 6, US 8) knitting needles

Stitch holder

Size:

To fit an average size adult head

Gauge (tension)

18 sts and 26 rows to 4in (10cm), using 5mm (UK 6, US 8) knitting needles and worsted (aran/10-ply) yarn, measured over stocking stitch.

Instructions:

Hat

Using 4mm (UK 8, US 6) needles and cream yarn, cast on 108 sts.

Row 1: (k1, p1) to end.

Rep row 1 seven times.

Change to 5mm needles and, beg with a knit row, work 34 rows in stocking stitch.

*Row 43: k1, sl1, k1, psso, k48, k2tog, k1, turn and leave rem sts on a holder.

Row 44: purl.

Row 45: knit.

Row 46: purl.

Row 47: k1, sl1, k1, psso, k to last 3 sts, k2tog, k1.

Row 48: purl.

Rep rows 47 and 48 until 44 sts rem.

Next row: k1, sl1, k2tog, psso, k to last 4 sts, k3tog, k1.

Next row: purl.

Rep last 2 rows three times more (28 sts).

Next row: k1, sl1, k2tog, psso, (k2tog) ten times, k3tog, k1 (14 sts).

Cast off purlwise.

Rejoin yarn to sts on holder and rep from * to end.

Ear (make 2)

Note that yarn is used double.

Using 5mm (UK 6, US 8) needles and two strands of black yarn, cast on 16 sts.

Row 1: k each st tbl.

Rep row 1 eleven times more.

Row 13: k1, sl1, k1, psso, k each st tbl to last 3 sts, k2tog, k1.

Row 14: k each st tbl.

Rows 15 and 16: as rows 13 and 14.

Rows 17, 18 and 19: as row 13.

Cast off rem 6 sts.

Cast off and cut yarn, leaving a long tail.

Eye patch (make 2)

Using 4mm (UK 8, US 6) needles and black yarn, cast on 8 sts.

Row 1: knit.

Row 2: inc1, k to last st, inc1.

Row 3–5: sl1, k to end.

Rep rows 2–5 twice more (14 sts).

Rows 14–20: sl1, k to end.

Row 21: k2tog, k to last 2 sts, k2tog.

Rows 22–24: sl1, k to end.

Rep rows 21–24 once more (10 sts).

Row 29: sl1, k to end.

Row 30: k2tog, k4, k2 tog.

Cast off rem 8 sts.

Nose

Using 4mm (UK 8, US 6) needles and black yarn, cast on 1 st.

Row 1: inc2 by knitting into front, back and front of st (3 sts).

Rows 2 and 3: sl1, k to end.

Row 4: inc1, k1, inc1 (5 sts).

Rows 5 and 6: sl1, k to end.

Row 7: inc1, k to last st, inc1.

Rep rows 5–7 twice more (11 sts).

Rows 14–18: sl1, k to end.

Cast off.

Making up

With right sides together and using the tail of yarn, stitch the side seam in backstitch. Neaten the ears, using the tails of yarn, then insert the straight edge of the ear into the centre of the sloping edge at each side. Pin it in place, then stitch the seam, trapping the ear between the layers. Turn right sides out. Stitch the eye patches in place on the front of the hat and stitch on the googly eyes. Stitch the nose in place, with the lower point at the top of the ribbed band. Add a small line of stitches below the nose.

SIMPLY BLUE BOOTEES

Instructions:

Make two.

Cast on 37 sts.

Row 1: knit.

Row 2: K1, *inc in next st, K15, inc in next st*, K1, rep from * to * once more, K1.

Row 3: knit.

Row 4: K2, *inc in next st, K15, inc in next st*, K3, rep from * to *, K2.

Row 5: knit.

Row 6: K3, *inc in next st, K15, inc in next st*, K5, rep from * to *, K3.

Row 7: knit.

Row 8: K4, *inc in next st, K15, inc in next st,* K7, rep from * to *, K4.

Row 9: knit.

Row 10: K5, *inc in next st, K15, inc in next st*, K9, rep from * to *, K5.

Row 11: knit.

Work ridge pattern as follows:

Row 12: knit.

Row 13: purl.

Row 14: knit.

Row 15: knit.

Row 16: purl.

Row 17: knit.

Rep rows 12–17 once.

Shape instep as follows:

Row 1: K33, sl1, K1, psso, turn.

Row 2: sl1, K9, P2tog, turn.

Row 3: sl1, K9, sl1, K1, psso, turn.

Rep rows 2 and 3 eight times.

Materials:
1 ball of fingering (4-ply) baby yarn in blue; 50g/191yd/175m

Needles:
1 pair of 3.75mm (UK 9, US 5) knitting needles

Rep row 2.

Next row: knit.

Work 3 more rows in GS, decreasing 1 st in centre of last row.

Work twisted rib as follows:

Next row: *K1tbl, P1*, rep from * to *.

Rep row 1 twenty times, cast off in rib.

Making up
Sew up the foot and back seams neatly. Turn over the ribbed top to form a cuff.

IMPERIUM BOOT CUFFS

Materials:

Three balls of super bulky (super chunky) yarn in blue; 100g/93yd/85m

Tools:

1 pair of 10mm (UK 000, US 15) circular needles, 23½in (60cm)

1 stitch marker

Instructions:

Make two.

Cast on 33sts loosely in blue. Place marker on right needle (this is to mark the beginning of the round).

Slip the first cast-on stitch to the left-hand needle, then knit this slipped stitch together with the last cast-on stitch. You will now have 32sts on your needle.

Remember to move the marker at the end of each round.

Rounds 1–24: *k1, p1* rep to the end of the row. Cast off sts loosly following rib pattern.

Weave in all loose ends.

A great simple pattern makes these cuffs perfect to keep feet snug while you are hard at work in the garden. Try making them in green to make a handsome complement to traditional rain (wellington) boots.

Grape expectations
The bobbly texture and wiggly vines make this a wonderfully tactile, playful cosy.

GRAPES TEA COSY

Gauge (tension)

5 sts = 1in (2.5cm).

Instructions:

Make two.

Using purple yarn and 4mm (UK 8, US 6) needles, cast on 42 sts.

Knit in SS until work measures 6in (15cm) from the cast-on edge.

Shape the top

Row 1: k7, k2tog, *k6, k2tog*, rep from * to * to last st, k1.

Row 2: purl.

Row 3: k6, k2tog, *k5, k2tog*, rep from * to * to last st, k1.

Row 4: purl.

Row 5: k5, k2tog, *k4, k2tog*, rep from * to * to last st, k1.

Row 6: purl.

Row 7: k4, k2tog, *k3, k2tog*, rep from * to * to last st, k1.

Row 8: purl.

Row 9: k3, k2tog, *k2, k2tog*, rep from * to * to last st, k1.

Row 10: purl.

Row 11: k2, k2tog, *k1, k2tog*, rep from * to * to last st, k1.

Row 12: purl.

Row 13: k1, k2tog, *k2tog*, rep from * to * to last st, k1.

Row 14: purl.

Row 15: change to green for stem and k1, k2tog, k1, k2tog, k1.

Row 16: purl.

Row 17: knit.

Row 18: purl.

Row 19: knit.

Cut yarn and place sts on stitch holder.

Materials:

One ball of worsted (aran/10-ply) yarn in purple and an oddment in green; 50g/98yd/90m

Needles:

1 pair of 4mm (UK 8, US 6) knitting needles and 1 pair of 4.5mm (UK 7, US 7) DPN

2 stitch holders

Making up

Place the wrong sides of the cosy together (right sides facing out). Thread a tapestry needle with the green tail on the back stitch holder. Graft the sts on the stitch holders together.

Sew the stem

Continuing with the green tail of yarn, sew down one side of the stem. Fasten off and hide tail in seam. Repeat on other side of stem.

Sew the top

Thread a tapestry needle with one of the purple tails at the top of the cosy. Sew down one side for 3in (7.5cm). Fasten off and hide tail in the seam.

Repeat on other side of cosy.

Sew the bottom

Thread a tapestry needle with one of the purple tails of yarn from the cast on edge.

Sew up one side for 1½in (4cm). Fasten off and hide tail in the seam.

Repeat on the other side of cosy.

Grapes (make about 34)

Using purple yarn and 4.5mm (UK 7, US 7) DPN, cast on 3 sts.

Row 1: kfb in each st.

Row 2: knit.

Row 3: k2tog across row.

Row 4: sk2po.

Cut yarn and pull through rem sts.

Using a tapestry needle and tails, sew grapes randomly on to cosy.

Vines (make six)

Using green yarn and 4.5mm (UK 7, US 7) DPN, cast on 24 sts.

Cast off the 24 sts.

Fasten off.

Twist vines to help make them curl.

Attach the vines

Position the vines to the base of the stem and sew in place. Weave in all loose ends.

GINGERBREAD HEART

Materials:

1 ball of fingering (4-ply) yarn in beige and a
  small amount in red; 50g/191yd/175m

Red felt or a button

Spare needle/stitch holder

Toy filling

Needles:

1 pair 3.25mm (UK 10, US 3) knitting needles

Size:

Approx. 2¾in (7cm) from top to point of heart
  (excluding hanging cord)

Instructions:

Heart shape (make 2)

∗ Cast on 3 sts and P 1 row.

Row 2: K1, M1, K1, M1, K1 (5 sts).

Row 3: P.

Row 4: K1, M1, K2, M1, K2 (7 sts).

Cut yarn and place sts on a spare needle or st holder.

Rep instructions from ∗ to make a second 'top' to your
heart. Do not cut yarn.

Place both pieces of knitting on the same needle with
WS facing.

Next row: P across both pieces (14 sts).

Work 2 rows in SS.

Next row: K2tog, K to last 2 sts, ssk (12 sts).

P 1 row.

Rep the last 2 rows a further four times until 4 sts rem.

Next row: K2tog, ssk (2 sts).

Next row: P2tog and fasten off rem st.

Making up

Place the hearts with wrong sides together and using
a darning needle and beige yarn, sew the hearts neatly
together, gently stuffing with toy filling as you go. Using
red fingering (4-ply) yarn, blanket stitch around the
edges of the heart. Attach a red felt heart or a button
in the centre of the heart with a cross stitch in beige
yarn. Repeat on the other side. Make a hanging cord by
twisting two strands of yarn together, one beige and
one red. Attach the cord to the top of the heart.

Sparkling Heart

*The alternative (opposite) features shimmering
white and pale blue yarn and a mother of pearl
heart button in the centre.*

These exotic novelty knits are great for decorating windowsills, whatever the season. For the alternative cactus, use an emerald green linen slub yarn and make up the flower in a red pure wool light worsted (DK/8-ply) yarn with a centre made from rainbow eyelash yarn.

CACTUS FLOWER

Materials:

- 1 ball of lace weight (2-ply) mohair yarn in pale green; 25g/219yd/200m
- Small amounts of light worsted (DK/8-ply) yarn in bright yellow and brown
- Oddment of novelty chenille thread in bright pink
- Flowerpot, 4in (10cm) in diameter
- Scrap of stiff card
- Toy stuffing
- Fabric glue or all-purpose adhesive (optional)

Needles:

Set of five 3mm (UK 11, US 2) DPN and 1 pair of 2.25mm (UK 13, US 1) knitting needles

Size:

2³⁄₈in (6cm) across and 3¹⁄₈in (8cm) high

Instructions:

Cactus

With mohair yarn and size 3mm (UK 11, US 2) DPN, cast on 8 sts and distribute between four needles.

Round 1: k.

Round 2: inc in each st (16 sts).

Round 3: (inc 1, k3) four times (20 sts).

Round 4: (inc 1, k4) four times (24 sts).

Round 5: (inc 1, k5) four times (28 sts).

Round 5: (inc 1, k6) four times (32 sts).

Knit 15 rounds without further increases.

Round 21: (k2tog, k6) four times (28 sts).

Knit 5 rounds.

Round 27: (k2tog, k5) four times (24 sts).

Knit 9 rounds.

Cast off; break yarn and fasten off.

Flower (in one piece)

With yellow yarn and size 2.25mm (UK 13, US 1) needles, cast on 9 sts.

Row 1: k all sts tbl.

Row 2: p6, turn.

Row 3: k to end.

Row 4: p.

Row 5: cast off 7 sts knitwise, k rem st.

Row 6: k2, cast on 7 sts.

Rep rows 1–6 four times more, then rep rows 1–4 once; cast off all sts knitwise; break yarn and fasten off.

Earth

With brown yarn used double and two size 3mm (UK 11, US 2) needles, cast on 8 sts.

Row 1: k.

Row 2: inc 1, k to end.

Rep last row until there are 20 sts.

Knit 8 rows without further increases.

Cast off 1 st at beg of next 12 rows.

Cast off rem 8 sts; break yarn and fasten off.

Making up

Cut a circle of stiff card 3½in (9cm) in diameter. Stitch a gathering thread all round the edge of the brown piece of knitting (earth), place the card circle centrally on the wrong side and pull up thread to gather; fasten off. Stuff the cactus firmly with polyester wadding. Using matching green yarn, stitch the base of the cactus to the earth. Bring the two edges of the flower petals together to make a circle and stitch the lower corners of the two end petals together; then run a gathering stitch along the base of the petals and pull up tightly to gather. Stitch a few strands of pink chenille thread in the centre of the flower, then stitch the flower in place on top of the cactus. Finally, wedge the whole thing into the top of a flower pot or small ornamental bucket; glue in place if you wish.

BARNEY COLLEGE BEAR

Materials:

1 ball each of light worsted (DK/8-ply) in grey, cream and deep turquoise; 50g/137yd/125m

Small amount of toy stuffing

2 x 6mm round black beads for eyes

Black embroidery thread or floss for features

Tools:

1 pair of 3.25mm (UK 10, US 3) knitting needles

Sewing needle

Stitch holder

Instructions:

Make the bear in grey yarn, following the pattern on page 41.

Sweatshirt (front)

Using cream, cast on 26 sts.

Rows 1–3: moss stitch.

Rows 4–5: SS.

Now place the motif, using the chart for guidance:

Row 6: K10, join in turquoise and K7, change back to cream and K9. This forms the base of the 'B'.

Rows 7–15: continue working from the chart until the motif is complete.

Rows 16–18: SS.

Rows 19–21: moss stitch.

Cast off.

Back

Work as front, but omit the motif.

Sleeves (make 2 the same)

Using cream, cast on 25 sts.

Rows 1–3: moss stitch.

Rows 4–5: SS.

Rows 6–7: join in turquoise, and SS.

Rows 8–9: SS using cream.

Rows 10–11: SS using turquoise.

Rows 12–13: SS using cream.

Cast off (this is the top of the sleeve).

Pants (make 2 pieces the same)

Using turquoise yarn, cast on 13 sts.

Rows 1–4: GS.

Rows 5–20: SS, ending on a purl row. Break yarn and leave these 13 sts on a spare needle.

Now work another piece to match. Do not break off yarn but continue as follows:

Knit across 13 sts on needle, cast on 2 sts, work across 13 sts left on spare needle (28 sts).

Next row: purl.

*Work a further 2 rows in SS, ending on a purl row.

Next row: K2, skpo, knit to last 4 sts, K2tog, K2.

Next row: purl.*

Repeat from * to * (24 sts).

Work 4 rows in rib, or as given in instructions.

Side stripe:

Using cream, cast on 20 sts.

Knit 1 row.

Cast off.

Making up

Work in the yarn ends on the sweatshirt, and stitch the shoulder seams for 5 sts in from each side. Fold the sleeves in half lengthways and mark the centre point at the top. Stitch them in place along the sides of the sweatshirt, matching the centre point to the shoulder seam. Now join the side and sleeve seams. Slip the sweatshirt over the bear's head. Join the trouser seams, stitch the stripe on to the side seam and put the trousers on to the bear.

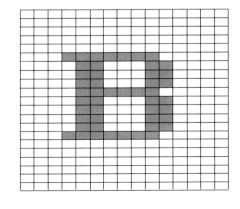

This big black cat is for all lovers of cats and those who believe that black cats are lucky.

BLACK CAT PHONE SOCK

Materials:

1 ball of light worsted (DK/8-ply) yarn in cream and small amounts in black, tan, green and white; 50g/131yd/120m

Black embroidery thread

Tools:

1 pair of 4mm (UK 8, US 6) and 1 pair of 3.5mm (UK 9, US 4) knitting needles

Embroidery needle

Scissors

Tape measure

Instructions:

Cat body

Using 4mm (UK 8, US 6) needles, cast on 6 stitches in black.

Row 1: knit.

Row 2: knit, inc 1 stitch at each end of row (8 sts).

Row 3: knit.

Rows 4 and 5: Rep rows 2 and 3 (10sts).

Rows 6–13: Work 8 more rows garter stitch.

Row 14: knit, dec 1 stitch at each end of row (6 sts).

Row 15: knit.

Row 16: k2tog to end (3sts).

Row 17: knit, inc in every stitch (6sts).

Row 18: knit.

Row 19: knit, inc 1st at each end of row (8 sts).

Rows 20–23: Work 4 rows garter stitch.

Rows 24–25: knit, dec 1 stitch at each end of rows (4 sts).

Row 26: k2, turn, knit 1 row (ear).

Row 27: k2tog, fasten off.

Repeat rows 26–27 for other ear.

Fasten off.

Cat tail

Using 4mm (UK 8, US 6) needles, cast on 16 sts in black.

Cast off.

Sock

Using 4mm (UK 8, US 6) needles, cast on 20 stitches and work stocking stitch until work measures 9½in (24cm).

Cast off.

Change to 3.5mm (UK 9, US 4) needles and pick up 20 sts at cosy top, rib 6 rows, cast off.

Repeat for the other end.

Fold the work in half, stitch the cat and tail in place with the embroidery needle and thread, then close the side seams.

Making up

Weave in the loose ends, then use the small amounts of green, white and tan yarn to embroider the face as shown.

Close the side seams using the cream yarn and mattress stitch.

This alternative design has been decorated with four colourful flowers. Work the stems and leaves in chain stitch, and then sew a flower button on to the top of each stem. These pretty mug hugs are perfect for keeping your drink hot during a well-deserved rest from tending the garden!

COTTAGE GARDEN MUG HUG

Materials:
1 ball each of light worsted (DK/8-ply) yarn
in green and blue, and small amounts
in various colours for embroidering the
flowers; 50g/131yd/120m

3 bee buttons

1 flower button

Needles:
1 pair of 4mm (UK 8, US 6)
knitting needles

Size:
Approx. 9¾ x 3¼in (25 x 8cm)

Instructions:

Using green yarn, cast on 43 sts.

Work 12 rows in GS.

Change to blue yarn and proceed in moss
stitch (US seed stitch) for 10 rows.

Change to GS and work 4 rows. Cast off.

Button edge
With RS facing and using blue yarn, pick up
and knit 17 sts evenly along one short edge.

Knit 1 row. Continue in GS.

Dec 1 st at each end of next and every alt row
until 7 sts rem. Cast off.

Buttonhole edge
Work other short edge in same way until 13 sts rem.

Next row: to make buttonhole, K2tog, K3, yrn twice,
K2tog, K2, K2tog.

Next row: knit, dropping the yrn of the previous row and
knitting into the loops.

Continue to dec as before until 7 sts rem. Cast off.

Making up
Embroider the flower stems on to the mug cosy using
green yarn and stem stitch. Add tiny flowers on the top
and sides of each stem using French knots. Sew the
bee buttons on to the flowers and add the flower button
at the opposite end to the buttonhole.

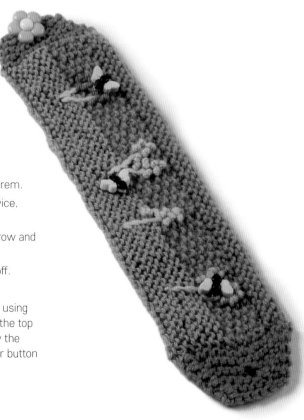

Materials:

1 ball of fingering (4-ply) yarn in beige and
small amounts in pink, orange and yellow;
50g/197yd/180m

1 ball of fluffy mohair/acrylic blend in cream;
25g/224yd/205m

Small amounts of light worsted (DK/8-ply) yarn
in red and mauve

Small amounts of cotton yarn in lime green

Black, red and pink seed beads

Jar lid for pastry case insert, approx.
3¼in (8cm) diameter

Toy stuffing

Needles:

1 pair of 3.25mm (UK 10, US 3) knitting needles
and 1 set of 4 x 2.25mm (UK 13, US 1) DPN

FRUIT TART

Instructions:

Tart case

Using beige fingering (4-ply) yarn, cast on 96 sts with 2.25mm (UK 13, US 1) DPN (32 sts on each of 3 needles).

Rounds 1–11: (K2, P2) for 11 rounds.

Round 12: purl.

Round 13: knit, decreasing 2 sts randomly on each needle.

Continue decreasing on each round until 1 st remains on each needle. Break yarn and pull through the remaining 3 sts.

Cream for inside tart

Using 3.25mm (UK 10, US 3) needles and cream, cast on 10 sts.

Rows 1–2: st st, starting with a K row.

Row 3: (K1, inc 1 st) five times across row (15 sts).

Row 4: purl.

Row 5: (K1, inc 1 st) to end (22 sts).

Row 6: purl.

Row 7: (K1, inc 1 st) to end (33 sts).

Row 8: purl.

Row 9: (K1, inc 1 st) to end (49 sts).

Rows 10–24: continue in st st.

Row 25: (K2tog, K1) to end (33 sts).

Row 26: purl.

Row 27: (K2tog, K1) to end (22 sts).

Row 28: purl.

Row 29: (K2tog, K1) to end (15 sts).

Row 30: purl.

Row 31: (K2tog, K1) to end (10 sts).

Row 32: purl.

Cast off.

Orange and lemon slices and raspberries

Make one orange slice, one lemon slice and three raspberries.

Using 3.25mm (UK 10, US 3) needles and appropriate colour, cast on 2 sts. Work in st st, starting with a K row.

Row 1: ∗ ∗ ∗ inc every st to end (4 sts).

Row 2: purl.

Row 3: inc every st to end (8 sts).

Row 4: purl. ∗

Row 5: inc every st to end (16 sts).

Row 6: purl. ∗∗

Cast off.

Berries and kiwi slices

Make eleven berries and two kiwi slices.

Using 3.25mm (UK 10, US 3) needles and mauve or lime green, cast on 2 sts and work as given for slices and raspberries from ∗ to ∗.

Row 5: K2tog to end (4sts).

Row 6: purl.

Row 7: K2tog to end (2sts).

Row 8: P2tog.

Break yarn and thread it through the last stitch.

Strawberries

Make two strawberries.

Cast on 2 sts using 3.25mm (UK 10, US 3) needles and red wool. Work 2 rows in st st.

Work as for slices and raspberries from ∗∗ to ∗∗.

Next row: inc every st to end (32 sts).

Starting with a P row, work in st st for 7 rows.

Cast off.

Making up

To finish each kiwi slice, stitch black seed beads in a circle on both sides. Sew up the side seam of each raspberry with right sides together – you will have a funnel shape. Turn right-side out. Insert a small ball of toy stuffing, pushing it well down into the raspberry. Use the same coloured wool to make a few criss-cross stitches just inside the raspberry – this will close in the stuffing and gather the top slightly. Decorate with pink seed beads. Sew up the side seam of each strawberry in the same way. Stuff completely, then gather the top and secure with a few stitches. Decorate with red seed beads. To finish a berry, gather up the knitted circle and secure the thread. Stitch five or six berries together to make a bunch. Secure the long thread in the middle of the tart case with a few stitches. Stretch the tart case over the jar lid. Lay a small amount of toy stuffing in the case then spread the knitted cream over the top, securing it at the edges with a few stitches. Arrange the fruit and secure through the cream with a few neat stitches.

The diminutive Pilquats are either very dark in colour, with striking blue antennae. or white and pink – but they both have cute faces.

PILQUAT ALIEN

Materials:

- 1 ball each of light worsted (DK/8-ply) yarn in cream and pink; 50g/137yd/125m
- 1 ball of bulky (chunky) multicoloured fluffy yarn; 100g/106yd/97m
- 2 beads for eyes

Small amount of red felt for mouth

Toy stuffing

Sewing needle and black thread

Needles:

1 pair of 3mm (UK 11, US 2) knitting needles

3mm crochet hook

Instructions:

Body (make 1)
Cast on 48 sts in multicoloured fluffy yarn.

Rows 1–7: st st.

Row 8: k2tog along row (24 sts).

Row 9: knit.

Row 10: k2tog along row (12 sts).

Row 11: knit.

Row 12: k2tog along row (6 sts).

Row 13: knit.

Row 14: k2tog along row (3 sts).

Row 15: purl. Cast off.

Head (make 1)
Cast on 24 sts in cream.

Rows 1–10: st st.

Row 11: k11, k inc in each of 2 next sts, k11 (26 sts).

Row 12: purl.

Row 13: k11, k2tog twice, k11 (24 sts).

Row 14: purl.

Row 15: k2tog along row (12 sts).

Row 16: purl.

Row 17: k2tog along row (6 sts).

Row 18: purl.

Row 19: k2tog along row (3 sts) and cast off.

Ears (make 2)
Cast on 4 sts in cream.

Rows 1–2: st st.

Row 3: k2tog (2 sts).

Row 4: p2tog cast off.

Legs (make 2)
Cast on 3 sts in pink.

Row 1: inc each st (6 sts).

Row 2: purl. Bring in cream yarn.

Rows 3–4: st st. Change to pink.

Rows 5–6: st st. Change to cream.

Rows 7–8: st st. Change to pink.

Rows 9–10: st st. Change to cream.

Rows 11–12: st st. Change to pink.

Rows 13–14: st st. Change to cream.

Rows 15–16: st st. Change to pink.

Rows 17–18: st st. Change to cream.

Rows 19–20: st st. Change to pink.

Rows 21–22: st st. Change to cream.

Rows 23–24: st st. Change to pink.

Rows 25–26: st st. Change to cream.

Rows 27–28: st st. Cast off.

Arms (make 2)
Cast on 2 sts in cream yarn.

Row 1: inc each st (4 sts).

Rows 2–17: st st.

Row 18: p2tog and cast off.

Making up
Sew up the centre back seams of the head and body. Turn each the right side out. Stuff the head and stitch it into the body cup. Needlesculpt the nose with a couple of stitches on either side of the bump. Sew up the the arms and legs with right sides out and stitch in place.

With the crochet hook, make two antennae from pink yarn. Crochet 7 chain stitches and cut a long thread. Thread this on to a tapestry needle and weave back through crocheted chain and insert into head of alien, secure with a couple of stitches, neaten thread and clip.

Stitch in place on the head. Finish by sewing on two beads as eyes, and making a little embroidered mouth.

Nestled in its protective leaves, the knobbly texture of the corn makes a fun and very recognisable novelty knit.

SWEETCORN

Instructions:

Corn (make 1)

With 3.25mm (UK 10, US 3) needles and yellow yarn, cast on 28 sts.

Row 1: k.

Row 2: p.

Row 3: k1, (k2tog) thirteen times, k1 (15 sts).

Row 4: k1, (M1, k1) thirteen times, k1 (28 sts).

Rows 5–44: Rep rows 1–4.

Row 45: cast off 2, k to end (26 sts).

Row 46: cast off 2, k to end (24 sts).

Rows 47–97: Cont in garter stitch (k every row).

Cast off.

Leaf (make 3)

With 2.75mm (UK 12, US 2) needles and light green yarn, cast on 27 sts.

Row 1: k3, (sl1 purlwise with yarn at back of work, k3) six times.

Row 2: p.

Rows 3–32: Rep rows 1 and 2 fifteen times.

Row 33: k1, sl1, k1, psso, (sl1 purlwise, k1, sl1, k1, psso) six times.

Row 34: p.

Row 35: k2, (sl1 purlwise, k2) six times.

Row 36: p.

Rows 37–42: Rep rows 35 and 36.

Row 43: k2tog, (sl1 purlwise, k2tog) six times (13 sts).

Row 44: p.

Row 45: k1, (sl1 purlwise, k1) six times.

Row 46: p.

Rows 47–52: Rep rows 45 and 46.

Row 53: k1, (k2tog) six times (7 sts).

Row 54: p.

Row 55: k.

Row 56: p.

Rows 57–60: Rep rows 55 and 56.

Row 61: k1, (sl1, k2tog, psso) twice (3 sts).

Row 62: p; cut yarn and thread through rem sts.

Materials:

- 1 ball of light worsted (DK/8-ply) cotton yarn in corn yellow; 50g/137yd/125m
- 1 ball of fingering (4-ply) wool or acrylic yarn in light green; 50g/197yd/180m
- Toy stuffing (optional)

Needles:

1 pair of 2.75mm (UK 12, US 2) and 1 pair of 3.25mm (UK 10, US 3) knitting needles

Knitting note

The instruction 'M1' requires you to make a stitch. To do this, pick up the strand in front of the next stitch to be worked, transfer it to the left-hand needle and knit into the back of the loop.

Making up

Starting at the cast-off edge, roll up the corn to form a firm cob, adding stuffing where necessary. Slipstitch the cast-on row to hold it in place. Pull up the stitches at the base of each leaf and stitch each one to the base of the corn cob, overlapping them slightly. The finished corn cob measures approximately 5 7/8in (15cm) long and 2½in (6.5cm) wide.

Fresh off the Boat

Real pineapples are delicious, and very good for you as they are full of vitamin C. This knitted one is simply very high in fibre!

Materials:

1 ball of light worsted (DK/8-ply) wool/cotton blend yarn in yellow; 50g/131yd/120m

1 ball of light worsted (DK/8-ply) bamboo blend yarn in green; 50g/104yd/95m

Toy stuffing

Sewing thread

Needles:

1 pair of 3.25mm (UK 10, US 3) and 1 pair of 2.75mm (UK 12, US 2) knitting needles

Size:

Approx. 4¾in (12cm) high and 10in (25cm) in circumference

PINEAPPLE

Instructions:

Pineapple (make 1)

With 3.25mm (UK 10, US 3) needles and yellow yarn, cast on 6 sts.

Row 1: k.

Row 2: (k1, inc1) three times (9 sts).

Row 3: k.

Row 4: k1, (inc2 in next st, k1) four times (17 sts).

Row 5: k.

Row 6: k2, (inc2 in next st, k3) three times, inc2 in next st, k2 (25 sts).

Row 7: k.

Row 8: k3, (inc2 in next st, k5) three times, inc2 in next st, k3 (33 sts).

Row 9: k.

Row 10: k4, (inc2 in next st, k7) three times, inc2 in next st, k4 (41 sts).

Row 11: k5, (p1, k9) three times, p1, k5.

Row 12: k4, (inc1, p1, inc1, k7) three times, inc1, p1, inc1, k4 (49 sts).

Row 13: k6, (p1, k11) three times, p1, k6.

Row 14: k5, (inc1, p1, inc1, k9) three times, inc1, p1, inc1, k5 (57 sts).

Pattern repeat

Rows 1 and 3: k.

Row 2: K1, *p3tog but do not transfer to right-hand needle, yon and p3tog again, k1, rep from * to end.

Row 4: k1, p1, k1, *p3tog but do not transfer to right-hand needle, yon and p3tog again, k1, rep from * to last 2 sts, p1, k1 (57 sts).

Work 4-row pattern repeat eight times:

Row 47: k1, (p3tog, k1) fourteen times (29 sts).

Row 48: k.

Row 49: k2, (k2tog, k4) four times, k2tog, k3 (26 sts).

Row 50: k.

Row 51: k2, (k2tog, k3) four times, k2tog, k2 (21 sts).

Row 52: k.

Row 53: k2, (k2tog, k2) five times (13 sts).

Row 54: k.

Row 55: k1, (k2tog, k1) four times.

Cut yarn, leaving a long tail, and thread through rem 9 sts.

Long leaf (make 7)

With 2.75mm (UK 12; US 2) needles and green yarn, cast on 7 sts.

Row 1: k2tog, yfwd, k1, p1, k1, yfwd, k2tog.

Row 2: k1, (p2, k1) twice.

Rep rows 1 and 2 seven times more.

Row 17: k2tog, k1, p1, k1, k2tog (5 sts).

Row 18: k1, (p1, k1) twice.

Row 19: k2, p1, k2.

Rep rows 18 and 19 twice more then row 18 once more.

Row 25: k2tog, p1, k2tog (3 sts).

Row 26: k3.

Row 27: k1, p1, k1.

Row 28: k3.

Row 29: sl1, k2tog, psso; fasten off.

Short leaf (make 5)

With 2.75mm (UK 12; US 2) needles and green DK (8-ply) yarn, cast on 7 sts.

Row 1: k2tog, yfwd, k1, p1, k1, yfwd, k2tog.

Row 2: k1, (p2, k1) twice.

Rep rows 1 and 2 four times more.

Continue as for long leaf from row 17 to end.

Making up

Join the edges of the pineapple with a neat backstitch seam, turning it right sides out and stuffing it firmly with toy stuffing before completing and closing the seam. Stitch the bases of leaves together to form a bundle, with the long leaves in the centre and the short leaves all around. Insert the base of the bundle into the top of the pineapple and stitch it firmly in place.

FLOSSIE HEADBAND

Instructions:

Flowers

Make five.

Using the colour of your choice, cast on 4 sts.

Row 1: k4.

Row 2: In the first st (k1, p1, k1tbl, p1, k1tbl), turn, k5, turn, p5, turn, k5, turn, p2tog twice, p1. Place the yarn to the back of your work, slip the second and third sts over the first stitch.

Row 3: Purl 3 remaining sts on left-hand needle.

Repeat rows 1–3 three times and then rows 1 and 2 once more. Cast off remaining sts purlwise.

Making up

Weave in all loose ends. Sew the cast-on edge and cast-off edge of each flower together. Sew one pompom in the centre of each flower.

Sew one flower in the centre of the length of jersey and space the other four 2¼in (6cm) apart across the front of the band. The two ends can be knotted together once the band is on your head.

This headband is reminiscent of spring flowers and bursts of colour after the winter months, and the flowers are quick and easy to make. The finished headband will fit a teenager or young adult, and can be easily adapted to fit any size.

These feminine wrist warmers are made in a fine mohair with a pretty border and ribbon edging.

LILAC WRIST WARMERS

Materials:

1 ball of of fingering (4-ply)
    yarn in variegated purple;
    100g/328yd/300m

39in (1m) narrow purple ribbon

Needles:

1 pair of 4mm (UK 8, US 6) and
1 pair of 3.25mm (UK 10, US 3)
knitting needles

1 cable needle

Instructions:

Bell border

Make two. Using 3.25mm (UK 10, US 3) needles, cast on 52 sts, then ktbl to form a neat edge.

Row 1 (RS): *p2, (k1, p1) four times, k1, p2*, rep from * to * to end of row.

Row 2: *k2, (p1, k1) four times, p1, k2*, rep from * to * to end of row.

Rows 3–4: Rep rows 1 and 2.

Row 5: *p2, k1, p1, ssk, k1, k2tog, p1, k1, p2*, rep from * to * to end of row (44 sts).

Row 6: *k2, p1, k1, p3, k1, p1, k2*, rep from * to * to end of row.

Row 7: *p2, k1, p1, sl2 knitwise, k1, pass the two slipped sts over one at a time, p1, k1, p2*, rep from * to * to end of row (36 sts).

Row 8: *k2, (p1, k1) twice, p1, k2*, rep from * to * to end of row.

Row 9: *p2, ssk, k1, k2tog, p2*, rep from * to * to end of row (28 sts).

Row 10: *k2, p3, k2*, rep from * to * to end of row.

Row 11: *p2, sl next three sts onto a cable needle, wrap yarn around the stitches twice, then knit the stitches from the cable needle, p2*, rep from * to * to end of row.

Row 12: *k2, p3, k2*, rep from * to * to end of row.

Change to 4mm (UK 8, US 6) needles.

Next row: *k4, inc1, k1, inc1*, rep from * to * to last 3 sts, knit to end of row (38 sts).

Next row: Purl.

Main pattern

Row 1: k2 *yfwd, k2tog* rep from * to * to last 2 sts, k2.

Row 2: Purl.

Continue working in st st until work measures 7¼in (18.5cm).

Change to 3.25mm (UK 10, US 3) needles.

Now rep rows 1 and 2 of main pattern.

Next row: k2tog, p1, *k1, p1*, rep from * to * to last 3 sts, k2tog, p1 (36 sts).

Next row: *k1, p1*, rep from * to * to end of row.

Cast off all sts.

Making up

With RS facing, join the side seams using a tapestry needle and mattress stitch, 2¾in (7cm) from the wrist end, starting after the bell border (the bell border will be left open) and 2⅜in (6cm) from the finger end. This will leave a gap for your thumb to go through. Weave in all loose ends.

Thread the ribbon though every other gap on the finger end, starting the threading at the centre front.
Tie the ribbon together with a bow.

PARISIENNE CHIC SCARF

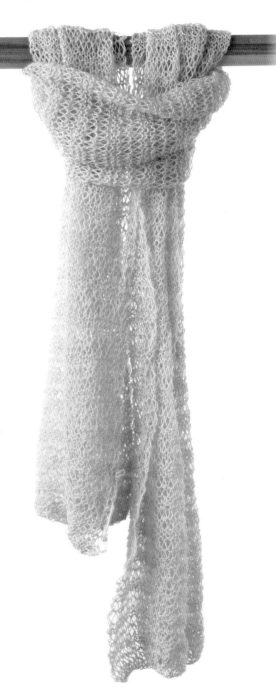

Instructions:

Initial rows
Rows 1–2: Cast on 56 sts, ktbl on return row
(i.e. row 2).

Scarf pattern
Rows 1–4: Knit.

Row 5: *k1, wyrn*, repeat from * to * until the last
stitch, k1.

Row 6: *k1, drop the stitch you wrapped in the previous
row*, repeat from * to * until the last stitch, k1.

Next rows: Repeat rows 1–6 until you have knitted
72½in (184cm), finishing with four rows of garter stitch.

Cast off sts.

Making up
Sew in all your loose ends by using a tapestry needle to
weave them into your knitting.

*This is a simple scarf that has been knitted in
a very fine lace yarn. You can drape it in many
ways and it will be a great asset to a spring or
summer wardrobe.*

ROLLED-UP BEANIE

Materials:

2 balls of light worsted (DK/8-ply) mohair blend yarn in pink; 50g/137yd/125m

Needles:

2 pairs of 4mm (UK 8, US 6) DPN

Size:

To fit a medium-large female adult head

Gauge (tension)

20 sts and 28 rows to 4in (10cm)
measured over stocking stitch.

Sweet as Candy

For a child-size version, use fingering (4-ply) yarn and 3mm (UK 11, US 3) needles, and follow the same pattern. For a beanie without the stalk on top, follow the pattern to the end of round 55, then cut the yarn, leaving a tail, thread the tail through the remaining 9 sts, pull up to close the gap and fasten off securely.

Instructions:

Cast on 108 sts and divide these sts between three of the needles, using the fourth to knit.

Knit 44 rounds.

Round 45: (k10, k2tog) nine times (99 sts).

Round 46: (k9, k2tog) nine times (90 sts).

Round 47: (k8, k2tog) nine times (81 sts).

Round 48: (k7, k2tog) nine times (72 sts).

Round 49: (k6, k2tog) nine times (63 sts).

Round 50: (k5, k2tog) nine times (54 sts).

Round 51: (k4, k2tog) nine times (45 sts).

Round 52: (k3, k2tog) nine times (36 sts).

Round 53: (k2, k2tog) nine times (27 sts).

Round 54: (k1, k2tog) nine times (18 sts).

Round 55: (k2tog) nine times (9 sts).

Row 56: (k3tog) three times (3 sts).

Transfer the rem 3 sts on to one needle and continue with two needles as follows:

Row 57: k3; do not turn but slide sts to other end of needle. Rep row 57 nine times more; cast off.

Weave in all loose ends.

BUMBLEBEE BOOTS

Materials:

1 ball each of fingering (4-ply) baby
   yarn in black and yellow, and an
   oddment in white; 50g/191yd/175m

Tools:

1 pair 3.75mm (UK 9, US 5)
   knitting needles

4mm (US 6, UK 8) crochet hook

Instructions:

Make two

Using black yarn, cast on 37 sts.

Rows 1–3: GS.

Join in yellow yarn and work the stripes in SS.

Rows 4–7: SS in yellow.

Rows 8–9: SS in black.

Rows 10–15: rep rows 4–9.

Rows 16–19: rep rows 4–7.

Break yellow.

Shape instep as follows:

Row 20: using black yarn, K24, turn.

Row 21: P11, turn.

Rows 22–25: join in yellow yarn and work 4 rows in SS.

Rows 26–27: join in black yarn and work 2 rows in SS.

Rows 28–31: join in yellow yarn and work 4 rows in SS.

Break yellow and continue in black only.

Rows 32–37: GS.

Break black.

Shape foot as follows:

With right-side facing, rejoin black yarn and pick up and knit 10 sts along first side of instep, 11 sts from instep, 10 sts along other side of instep, and knit across rem 13 sts (57 sts).

Work 15 rows in GS.

Next row: K1, *K2togtbl, K23, K2tog, K1*, rep from * to * to end of row.

Next row: knit.

Next row: K1, *K2togtbl, K21, K2tog, K1*, rep from * to * to end of row.

Next row: knit.

Next row: K1, *K2togtbl, K19, K2tog, K1*, rep from * to * to end of row.

Next row: knit.

Cast off.

Making up

Work in all the ends neatly. Join the foot and leg seams, matching the stripes as you do so. Using black yarn, make two pairs of antennae. For each pair, make a knitted cord by casting on 24 sts, then casting off. Work in the ends. Using a crochet hook, pull each end of one knitted cord through to the front of a bootee, positioning them as shown in the picture, and secure the cord in the centre on the inside of the bootee. Curl each end of the antennae into a tiny ball and secure with a few stitches. Embroider the eyes and mouth using white and black yarn, using the picture for guidance.

Two hanks of variegated worsted (aran/10-ply) yarn were used for this version of the boot cuffs. Even a simple change in colour can alter the character of your projects, so have fun experimenting.

HEMINGWAY BOOT CUFFS

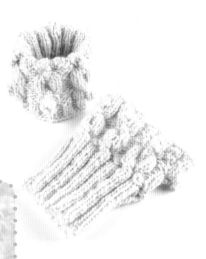

Materials:

2 balls of worsted (aran/10-ply) textured yarn in cream (women's) or variegated (men's); 50g/104yd/95m

Needles:

1 pair of 5mm (UK 6, US 8) and 1 pair of 6mm (UK 4, US 10) knitting needles

Cable needle

Instructions:

Women's (make 2)

Using 5mm (UK 6, US 8) needles, cast on 52sts in cream yarn.

Rows 1–21: work rows in k2/p2 rib.

Row 22: Using set rib pattern, increase on second and every following twelfth st. (56sts)

Men's (make 2)

Using 5mm (UK 6; US 8)needles, cast on 60sts in variegated yarn.

Rows 1–25: work rows in k2/p2 rib.

Row 26: Inc 1 on every fifth st. (72sts)

Change to 6mm (UK 4; US 10) needles and insert knotted cable as follows:

Knotted cable section

This is worked over 6 sts on a background of reverse st st.

Cable block: (RS) k2, p2, k2

Rows 1, 5, 7 and 9 (women's): p3, *insert cable block, p3* rep from * to * until last 8sts, insert cable block, p2.

Rows 1, 5, 7 and 9 (men's): p2, *insert cable block, p3* rep from * to * until last 7sts, insert cable block, p1.

Row 2 and all even rows to row 10 (women's): k2, *p2, k2, p2, k3*. Rep from * to * to the end of the row.

Row 2 and all even rows to row 10: (men's): k1, *insert cable block, k3* rep from * to * to last 8 st, insert cable block, k2.

Row 3: p3, *cable 6 – slip next 4 sts on to cable needle and hold at front of work, knit next 2 sts from left-hand needle, then slip the 2 purl sts from the cable needle back to the left-hand needle. Pass the cable needle with 2 rem knit sts to the back of work, purl sts from left-hand needle, then knit the sts from the cable needle; p3* rep until last 8sts, repeat cable block once more, p2.

Rows 11–14: As rows 1–4 of set pattern.

Bobble row

Row 15 (women's): p3 *k2, MB, p1, k2, p3*, rep from * to * until last 8 sts, insert cable block, p2.

Row 15 (men's): p2 *insert cable block, p1, MB, p1*, rep from * to * until last 7sts, insert cable block, p1.

Remember to knit into the bobble stitch again before continuing with the pattern.

Row 16: As row 2.

Row 17: *k2, p2* rep from * to * until the end of row.

Row 18: Cast off sts.

Making up

Using a tapestry needle, sew in all of the ends. With right side facing, use a mattress stitch to join the side seams of the pattern component of the boot cuff. Sew up the rib on the rear side of the boot cuff.

Making a bobble

MB: To make bobble, (k1, yo, k1, yo, k1) into next st, turn and p5, turn and k1, sl1, k2tog, psso, k1, turn and p3tog. With right side facing, knit into the bobble st again.

Tea By the Sea

This gorgeous cosy would add a cute finishing touch to a vintage tea party.

Materials:

1 ball each of worsted (aran/10-ply) yarn in
  navy and white, and an oddment in red;
  50g/93yd/85m

Tools:

1 pair of 4mm (UK 8, US 6) knitting needles and
  1 pair of 4.5mm (UK 7, US 7) DPN

2 stitch holders

Gauge (tension)

5 sts = 1in (2.5cm).

NAUTICAL TEA COSY

Instructions:

Make two.

Using navy yarn and 4mm (UK 8, US 6) needles, cast on 42 sts.

Work 16 rows in SS.

Change to white yarn and work 8 rows.

Change to navy yarn and work 8 rows.

Change to white yarn and work 8 rows.

Change to navy yarn and work 8 rows.

Change to white yarn and work 2 rows.

Shape the top

Row 1: continue with white yarn, k7, k2tog, *k6, k2tog*, rep from * to * to last st, k1.

Row 2: purl.

Row 3: k6, k2tog, *k5, k2tog*, rep from * to * to last st, k1.

Row 4: purl.

Row 5: k5, k2tog, *k4, k2tog*, rep from * to * to last st, k1.

Row 6: purl.

Row 7: k4, k2tog, *k3, k2tog*, rep from * to * to last st, k1.

Row 8: purl.

Row 9: k3, k2tog, *k2, k2tog*, rep from * to * to last st, k1.

Row 10: purl.

Row 11: change to navy yarn and k2, k2tog, *k1, k2tog*, rep from * to * to last st, k1.

Row 12: purl.

Row 13: k1, k2tog, *k2tog*, rep from * to * to last st, k1.

Row 14: purl.

Row 15: change to red yarn and k1, k2tog, k1, k2tog, k1.

Row 16: purl.

Row 17: knit.

Repeat rows 16 and 17 until 'knot' measures 6in (15cm).

Cut yarn and place sts on stitch holder.

Making up

Place the wrong sides of the cosy together (right sides facing out). Thread a tapestry needle with the red tail on the back stitch holder. Graft the sts on the stitch holders together.

Sew the top red section

Continuing with the red tail of yarn, sew down one side of the red section. Fasten off and hide tail in seam. Repeat on other side of the red section.

Sew the top

Thread a tapestry needle with one of the navy tails at the top of the cosy. Sew down one side for 7.5cm (3in). Fasten off and hide tail in the seam. Repeat on other side of cosy.

Sew the bottom

Thread a tapestry needle with one of the navy tails of yarn from the cast-on edge. Sew 4cm (1½in) up one side. Fasten off and hide tail in the seam. Repeat on the other side of cosy. Tie the red tail in a knot on the top of the cosy.

Life ring

Using white yarn and the 4.5mm (UK 7, US 7) DPN, cast on 4 sts.

Row 1: *k4; do not turn but slide sts to other end of needle*, rep from * to * seven times.

Change to red yarn.

Row 2: *k4; do not turn but slide sts to other end of needle*, rep from * to * three times.

Change to white.

Repeat rows 1–2 three times.

(Note: carry red and white yarn up the back of the life ring as you knit).

Fasten off and sew together to form ring. Work in ends neatly.

The string

Using red yarn and 4.5mm (UK 7, US 7) DPN, cast on 2 sts.

Row 1: k2; do not turn but slide sts to other end of needle.

Repeat this row until work measures approximately 2½in (6.5cm).

Fasten off.

Using one of the tails, sew string to the top of the life ring. With the other tail, sew string below the knot. Work in all loose ends.

A Very Mini Christmas!
These tiny stockings make perfect tree decorations, or you could put them out as table presents, filled with miniature gifts.

MINI CHRISTMAS STOCKING

Materials:

Small amount of fingering (4-ply) yarn in red,
cream and gold

Toy stuffing

Tools:

1 pair of 3.25mm (UK 10, US 3) knitting needles

3.25mm (US D-3) crochet hook (optional)

Size:

Approx. 2½in (6.5cm) tall

Instructions:

Stocking

Using red yarn, cast on 12 sts.

Row 1 (WS): P5, PM, P2, PM, P5.

Row 2: Cast on 4 sts, K to M, M1, SM, K2, SM, M1, K to
end of row (18 sts).

Row 3: Cast on 4 sts, P to M, M1, SM, P2, SM, M1, P to
end of row (24 sts).

Row 4: Cast on 6 sts, K to M, M1, SM, K2, SM, M1, K to
end of row (32 sts).

Row 5: Cast on 6 sts, P to M, M1, SM, P2, SM, M1, P to
end of row (40 sts).

Row 6: K to M, M1, SM, K2, SM, M1, K to end of row
(42 sts).

Starting with a P row, work 3 rows in SS.

Next row: K to 2 sts before M, ssk, SM, K2, SM, K2tog, K
to end of row (40 sts).

Next row: P to 2 sts before M, ssp, SM, P2, SM, P2tog, P
to end of row (38 sts).

Rep the last 2 rows three more times until 26 sts rem.

Remove markers and work 12 rows in SS.

Change to cream and work 11 rows in GS.

Change to gold yarn and K1 row.

Cast off as follows (picot cast off):

* Cast on 2 sts, cast off 5 sts, pass st back to left-hand
needle. Rep from * to the last 2 sts, cast off these sts.
Fasten off yarn.

Hanging loop

Using the crochet hook and cream yarn, make 12
chain sts. Fasten off and attach to the back of the cuff.
Alternatively, braid a length of yarn to make the loop.

Making up

Sew the stocking's side seam, bearing in mind that the
GS top will fold over so the WS will show. Sew in the
ends. Attach the loop inside the stocking at the back
after folding the top over. Stuff a little toy filling into
the stocking.

Hyacinths could be used singly or in a bunch, as a lapel pin on a jacket. Use a textured, variegated yarn in pink/purple for an alternative; if it is slightly thicker, the resulting flower will be larger, even if you use the same size needles.

GRAPE HYACINTH

Materials:

Small amount of fingering (4-ply) silk yarn in bright
   purple

Small amount of light worsted
   (DK/8-ply) pure wool yarn in green

Needles:

1 pair of 3.25mm (UK 10, US 3) knitting needles
   and 1 pair of 3mm (UK 11, US 2) DPN

Size:

Approx. 5¾in (14.5cm) long,
   including stem

Special stitch

To make a bobble (mb): Knit into front, back and front of
stitch, turn; k3, turn; k3, turn; pass 2nd and 3rd stitches
over 1st stitch, then slip this stitch back on to right-hand
needle; turn.

*To make a lapel pin, use matching yarn to
stitch a brooch pin to the slip-stitched seam.*

Instructions:

Flower

With silk yarn and 3.25mm (UK 10, US 3) needles, cast
on 15 sts.

Row 1: *mb, k3, rep from * to end.

Row 2: p.

Row 3: k2, (mb, k3) four times, k1.

Row 4: p .

Rep rows 1–4 once, then rep rows 1 and 2 once; cast off
all sts knitwise; break yarn and fasten off.

Stem

With green yarn and two DPN, cast on 2 sts.

Row 1: k2; do not turn but slide sts to other end
of needle.

Rep this row until work measures 2½in (6.5cm).
Fasten off.

Making up

Place the cast-off edge of the flower over the cast-on
edge, overlapping slightly, and slip stitch it in place.
Stitch the three bobbles at the top of the flower
together in a cluster. Insert the end of the stem into the
base of the flower and stitch it in place.

OLIVIA SWEETHEART BEAR

Materials:

1 ball each of light worsted (DK/8-ply) yarn in pale pink, cream and pink; 50g/137yd/125m

Small piece of narrow pink ribbon

Small quantity of toy stuffing

2 x 6mm round black beads for eyes

Black embroidery thread or floss for features

Tools:

1 pair of 3.25mm (UK 10, US 3) knitting needles

Sewing needle

Stitch holder

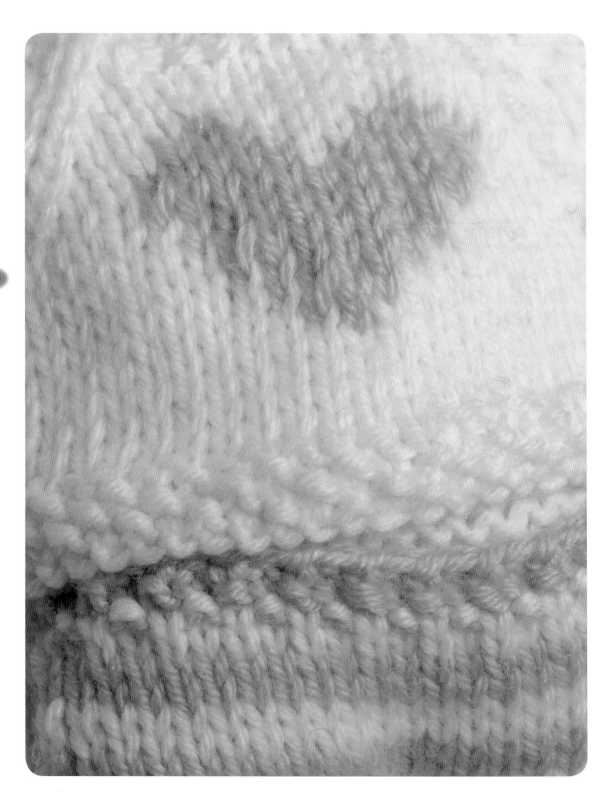

Instructions:

Make the bear using pink yarn following the instructions on page 41.

Trousers (make 2 pieces the same)

Work the first 4 rows of the trouser legs in moss stitch using pink, and the remainder of the trousers in SS stripes of 2 rows cream and 2 rows pink. The waistband is worked in moss stitch.

Using pink yarn and 3.25mm (UK 10; US 3) needles, cast on 13 sts.

Rows 1–4: moss stitch.

Rows 5–20: SS, ending on a purl row and following colour theme, as above. Break yarn and leave these 13 sts on a spare needle.

Now work another piece to match. Do not break off yarn but continue as follows:

Knit across 13 sts on needle, cast on 2 sts, work across 13 sts left on spare needle (28 sts).

Next row: purl.

*Work a further 2 rows in SS, ending on a purl row.

Next row: K2, skpo, knit to last 4 sts, K2tog, K2.

Next row: purl.*

Repeat from * to * (24 sts).

Work 4 rows in rib, or as given in instructions.

Sweater (back)

Using cream, cast on 25 sts.

Rows 1–4: moss stitch.

Rows: 5–10: SS.

To shape armholes:

Rows 11–12: continue in SS, and cast off 2 sts at beg of each row.

Row 13: K1, skpo, knit to last 3 sts, K2tog, K1.

Row 14: purl.

Repeat rows 13 and 14 until 9 sts remain, ending with a purl row. Leave sts on a stitch holder.

Sleeves (make 2 the same)

Using cream, cast on 25 sts.

Rows 1–4: moss stitch.

Rows 5–8: SS.

Shape top as for back.

Front

Using cream, cast on 25 sts.

Rows 1–4: moss stitch.

Rows 5–8: SS.

Now place the heart motif, working from the chart.

Row 9: K12, join in pink and K1, change back to cream and K12.

Rows 10–17: continue to follow chart, and shape armholes as for back.

When 15 sts rem, divide for neck:

Row 18: K1, skpo, K2, turn and leave rem sts on a stitch holder.

Row 19: purl.

Row 20: K1, skpo, K1.

Row 21: purl.

Row 22: K3tog.

Fasten off.

Slip first 5 sts on to safety pin for centre neck, join yarn to remaining sts and complete to match back, reversing the shaping and working K2tog in place of skpo.

Neckband

Using cream, work in moss stitch. Pick up and knit sts across top of sleeve, 5 sts on left side of front, 5 sts across centre, 5 sts on right side of front, across back neck and across top of other sleeve (42 sts).

Moss stitch for 3 rows. Cast off.

Making up

Sew up the trousers, matching the stripes. Sew up the sweater and slip it over the bear's head before joining the final raglan seam and neckband. Complete the sewing up. Make a small pink bow and stitch it on to the bear's head.

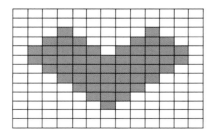

The surface of this phone sock (see detail) is seersucker stitch, which helps to give textural interest to the piece. This sock is aimed at those with an intermediate level of knitting expertise.

FUNKY ORANGE PHONE SOCK

Materials:

1 ball of light worsted (DK/8-ply) yarn in burnt orange; 50g/137yd/125m

1 novelty heart button

14in (36cm) of sequinned ric-rac braiding

Orange embroidery thread

Tools:

1 pair of 4.5mm (UK 7, US 7) knitting needles

3.25mm (UK 10, US D) crochet hook

Sewing needle

Scissors

Tape measure

Instructions:

Using 4.5mm (UK 7, US 7) needles, cast on 32 sts in burnt orange.

Row 1: (RS) k1 (edge) *k1, p1, k1, p1*; rep from * to * to last 2 sts, k1, k1.

Row 2: work each st as it presents (see page 7).

Row 3: k1, *p1, k3*; rep from * to * to last 2 sts, p1, k1.

Row 4: work each st as it presents.

Row 5: (RS) k1 (edge) *k1, p1, k1, p1*; rep from * to * to last 2 sts, k1, k1.

Row 6: work each st as it presents.

Row 7: k1, *k2, p1, k1*, rep from * to * to last 2 sts, k1, k1.

Row 8: work each st as it presents.

Next rows: Rep rows 1–8 until work measures 5in (13cm).

Cast off 16 sts.

Change to garter stitch (all knit rows) for 2in (5cm).

On last row, cast off 8 sts then slip the one stitch on the RH needle on to the crochet hook and chain 6 detached chain stitches, slip the last stitch back on to the RH knitting needle and cast off remaining stitches.

Making up

Close the side seams using mattress stitch. Use the needle and thread to attach the button, then the ric-rac braiding as a handle.

Add a touch of luxury to your creamy coffee with these sumptuous cosies. The alternative version is worked in black.

COFFEE AND CREAM MUG HUG

Materials:

1 ball of light worsted (DK/8-ply) yarn in coffee; 50g/137yd/125m

Oddment of textured yarn in cream

1 wooden button

Needles:

1 pair of 4mm (UK 8, US 6) knitting needles

Size:

Approx. 10¼ x 3¼in (26 x 8cm)

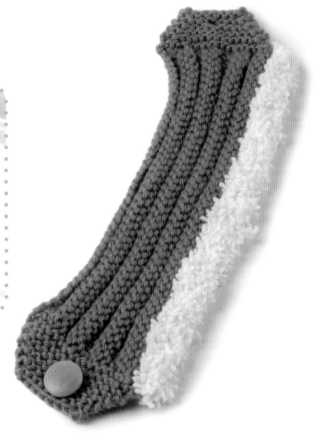

Instructions:

Cast on 44 sts using coffee-coloured yarn.

Row 1: (RS facing) knit.

Row 2: purl.

Row 3: knit.

Row 4: knit.

Row 5: purl.

Row 6: knit.

Rep rows 1–6 three times.

Change to cream textured yarn and work 8 rows in GS.

Cast off.

Button edge

With RS facing and coffee-coloured yarn, pick up and knit 17 sts evenly along one short edge.

Knit 1 row.

Continue in GS.

Dec 1 st at each end of next and every alt row until 7 sts rem. Cast off.

Buttonhole edge

Work along the other short edge in the same way until 11 sts rem.

Next row: to make buttonhole, K2tog, K3, yrn twice, K2tog, K2, K2tog.

Next row: knit, dropping the yrn of the previous row and knitting into the loops.

Continue to dec as before until 7 sts rem.

Cast off.

Making up

Work in all ends neatly. Sew on the wooden button to correspond with the buttonhole at the other end.

JAZZY CAKE

Instructions:

Iced top

Cast on 10 sts in off-white.

Rows 1–15: work in st st, starting with a K row,
increasing 1 st at beg and end of each K row (26 sts).

Row 16: purl.

Row 17: knit.

Row 18: purl.

Rows 19–33: continue in st st, decreasing 1 st at beg
and end of each K row (10 sts).

Row 34: purl.

Cast off.

Side of cake

Using multicoloured light worsted (DK/8-ply) yarn,
cast on 17 sts.

Rows 1–90: st st.

Cast off.

*The fun pink and green jazzy cake has a green
cherry on the top. To make it, cast on 5 sts
and work 5 rows in st st. Cast off. Make a row
of gathering stitches around the edge of
the knitted berry, add a small amount of toy
stuffing to the centre, then pull up the thread
and secure.*

Base of cake

Using multicoloured light worsted (DK/8-ply) yarn, cast
on 8 sts.

Rows 1–2: work in st st, starting with a K row.

Row 3: knit, increasing 1 st at beg and end of row
(10 sts).

Row 4: purl.

Row 5: knit, increasing 1 st at beg and end of row
(12 sts).

Rows 6–10: continue in st st.

Row 11: knit, decreasing 1 st at beg and end of row
(10 sts).

Row 12: purl.

Row 13: knit, decreasing 1 st at beg and end of row
(8 sts).

Row 14: purl.

Cast off.

Making up

Make small ridges going widthways across the side of
the cake, holding them in place with rows of running
stitches. Stitch the short edges of the cake side
together to form a tube. Sew the cake base to one
end. Fill with stuffing. Sew the iced top in place. Using
the fluffy acrylic yarn, make a row of running stitches
around the edge of the icing. Decorate the top with
multicoloured yarn oddments and beads. Tie a ribbon
around the cake and make a small bow at the front.

The strange-looking Grosperneatts have very horn-like antennae and long tentacles to anchor themselves to the rocks.

GROSPERNEATT ALIEN

Instructions:

Body
Cast on 10 sts in light brown.

Row 1: inc each st (20 sts).

Row 2: purl.

Row 3: inc each st (40 sts).

Rows 4–16: st st.

Row 17: *k1, k2tog* rep from * to * to end.

Rows 18–20: st st.

Row 21: *k1, k2tog* rep from * to * to end.

Row 22: purl. Cast off.

Horns (make 2)

Cast on 3 sts in cream.

Row 1: inc each st (6 sts).

Row 2: purl..

Rows 3–31: st st.

Row 32: k2tog (3 sts).

Row 33: purl. Cast off.

Making up
Fold the body in half with right sides facing. Sew up the centre back seam, leaving the bottom end open. Turn it the right side out, then stuff and stitch closed. Needlesculpt the nose and sew on beads for eyes. Sew the horns along their whole length, right side out. Position them on the head and stitch in place. Curl horns and stitch them into the desired shape.

Tentacles (make 4)
Using the multicoloured fluffy yarn, cast on and k1; inc into this (2 sts), then work in st st until the work reaches the desired length and p2tog. Cast off. Thread the tail of yarn on to a tapestry needle and weave it back through tentacle. This gives it a bit more body. You can shape the tentacle into a curve by pulling slightly on it. If enough thread is left over, you can use it to secure the tentacle to your alien.

Antennae (make 2)
With a 3mm crochet hook and brown yarn, crochet 7 chains and cut a long thread. Thread this on to a tapestry needle and weave back through the crocheted chain. Stitch each one either side of the mouth area and fasten off.

Materials:
1 ball each of light worsted (DK/8-ply) yarn in light brown and cream; 50g/137yd/125m

1 ball of multicoloured fluffy yarn; 100g/106yd/97m

Small amount of brown yarn for mouth

2 beads for eyes

Toy stuffing

Black sewing thread

Tools:
1 pair 3mm (UK 11, US 2) knitting needles

3mm crochet hook

Sewing needle

PUMPKIN

Materials:

1 ball each of light worsted (DK/8-ply) pure wool yarn in orange and lime green; 50g/137yd/125m

Toy stuffing

Needles:

Set of five 3.25mm (UK 10, US 3) DPN and 1 pair of 3.25mm (UK 10, US 3) knitting needles

Size:

Approx. 4in (10cm) wide and 2⅛in (5.5cm) high (excluding stalk)

Instructions:

Pumpkin

With set of five 3.25mm (UK 10, US 3) DPN and orange yarn, cast on 16 sts and distribute these equally between four needles.

Round 1: k.

Round 2: (inc1, k1) eight times (24 sts).

Round 3: (inc1, k1, p1) eight times (32 sts).

Round 4: (inc1, k2, p1) eight times (40 sts).

Round 5: (inc1, k3, p1) eight times (48 sts).

Round 6: (inc1, k4, p1) eight times (56 sts).

Round 7: (inc1, k5, p1) eight times (64 sts).

Round 8: (inc1, k6, p1) eight times (72 sts).

Round 9: (k8, p1) 8 times.

Rounds 10–19: Rep round 9.

Round 20: (k7, k2tog) eight times (64 sts).

Round 21: (k6, k2tog) eight times (56 sts).

Round 22: (k5, k2tog) eight times (48 sts).

Round 23: (k4, k2tog) eight times (40 sts).

Round 24: (k3, k2tog) eight times (32 sts).

Round 25: (k2, k2tog) eight times (24 sts).

Round 26: (k1, k2tog) eight times (16 sts).

Round 27: k2tog eight times.

Break yarn and thread through rem 8 sts.

Stalk

With green yarn and pair of size 3.25 mm (UK 10, US 3) needles, cast on 2 sts.

Row 1: k both sts tbl.

Row 2 and every even-numbered row: k.

Row 3: cast on 2, k to end (4 sts).

Row 5: cast on 3, k to end (7 sts).

Row 7: cast off 3, k to end (4 sts).

Row 9: cast off 2, k to end (2 sts).

Row 10: k.

Rows 11–34: Rep rows 3–10 three times.

Rows 35–36: Rep rows 1–9 (2 sts).

Row 37: cast on 6 sts, k to end (8 sts).

Rows 38–44: k.

Cast off and break yarn, leaving a long tail.

Making up

Pull up the stitches on the last row of the pumpkin and fasten off securely; this forms the base of the pumpkin. Insert stuffing through the hole formed by the cast-on edge. Fill the pumpkin fairly tightly but do not over-stuff or it will become stretched out of shape. Thread a tapestry needle with orange yarn, then thread through stitches around the hole in the top of the pumpkin and pull up. Roll up the stalk and, with the tail of green yarn, stitch the side edges of the stalk and leaves together, then stitch the stalk to the top of the pumpkin.

The Grapes of Fluff

Delicious grapes are even better if you can convince someone to peel them and feed them to you.

BUNCH OF GRAPES

Materials:

- 1 ball of fingering (4-ply) wool or wool blend yarn in purple; 50g/191yd/175m
- Small amount of light worsted (DK/8-ply) wool yarn in brown
- Toy stuffing

Tools:

1 pair of 2.25mm (UK 13, US 1) knitting needles and 1 pair of 3mm (UK 11, US 2) DPN

Size:

Approx. 5⅛in (13cm) excluding stalk

Instructions:

Large grape (make 7)

With 2.25mm (UK 13, US 1) needles and purple yarn, cast on 6 sts.

Row 1 and all odd-numbered (WS) rows until row 19: p.

Row 2: inc1 in each st (12 sts).

Row 4: (k1, inc1) six times (18 sts).

Row 6: (k2, inc1) six times (24 sts).

Beg with a p row, work 7 rows in st st (1 row p, 1 row k).

Row 14: (k2, k2tog) six times (18 sts).

Row 16: (k1, k2tog) six times (12 sts).

Row 18: (k2tog) six times (6 sts).

Row 19: (p2tog) three times; cut yarn, leaving a tail, and thread through rem 3 sts.

Small grape (make 9)

With 2.25mm (UK 13, US 1) needles and purple yarn, cast on 6 sts.

Row 1 and all odd-numbered (WS) rows until row 13: p.

Row 2: inc1 in each st (12 sts).

Row 4: (k1, inc1) six times (18 sts).

Beg with a p row, work 5 rows st st.

Row 10: (k1, k2tog) six times (12 sts).

Row 12: (k2tog) six times (6 sts).

Row 13: (p2tog) three times; cut yarn, leaving a tail, and thread through rem 3 sts.

Stalk (make 1)

With 3.00mm (UK 11, US 2) DPN and brown yarn, cast on 4 sts.

Row 1: k4; do not turn but slide sts to other end of needle.

Rep row 1 twelve times more, then turn and cast on 3 sts (7 sts).

Row 14: k to end, turn and cast on 3 sts (10 sts).

Row 15: k.

Cast off.

Making up

Graft the edges of each grape together and stuff firmly. Pull up the tail of yarn to pull the stitches on the last row together. Make a cluster of three small grapes by passing a tail of yarn through one end of each, then pulling it up tightly before fastening it off. Thread a tapestry needle with two strands of purple fingering (4-ply) yarn, then join the end of the yarn to one end of one small grape and pass the needle up through the centre of the cluster of three grapes.

Make another cluster in the same way, this time of five small grapes, and pass the needle up through the centre. Make a cluster of four large grapes and pass the needle up through the centre; then a cluster of three large grapes; fasten the yarn firmly to the centre of this cluster. Finally, pass the needle through the end of the stalk and stitch it firmly in place. On the top (cast-off) edge of the stalk, fold over the cast-off row and oversew using matching yarn.

This neat, decorative headband is great for all ages. Simply knit it to the length required (it should fit snugly around the head with a bit of stretch) and add a pretty button as a detail.

GOOSEBERRY HEADBAND

Materials:

1 ball of light worsted (DK/8-ply) merino/
   alpaca yarn in gooseberry; 50g/124yd/113m
2 x buttons

Needles:

1 pair of 4mm (UK 8, US 6) knitting needles

Instructions:

Cast on 9 sts and ktbl in every st.

Row 1 (buttonhole row): k4, cast off 2 sts, knit to end.

Row 2: k3, cast on 2 sts using cable cast on method, k4.

Row 3: inc1, knit to last st, inc1 (11 sts).

Row 4: p1, *yrn, p2tog, rep from * to end.

Repeat rows 3 and 4 until there are 17 sts.

Lace pattern

Row 1 (RS): sl1, yfrn, k3, sl1, k1, psso, p5, k2tog, k3, yfrn, k1.

Row 2: sl1, p5, k5, p6.

Row 3: sl1, k1, yfrn, k3, sl1, k1, psso, p3, k2tog, k3, yfrn, k2.

Row 4: sl1, p6, k3, p7.

Row 5: sl1, k2, yfrn, k3, sl1, k1, psso, p1, k2tog, k3, yfrn, k3.

Row 6: sl1, p7, k1, p8.

Row 7: sl1, k3, yfrn, k3, sl1, k2tog, psso, k3, yfrn, k4.

Row 8: sl1, purl to last st.

Repeat the last 8 rows until work measures 18in (46cm) or desired length, and is long enough to go around your head with a slight stretch (ending on a row 8).

Row 1: k1, k2tog, knit to last 3 sts, k2tog, k1 (15 sts).

Row 2: p1, *yfrn, p2tog, rep from * to end.

Repeat the last 2 rows until there are 9 sts.

Next row: Knit.

Cast off all sts.

Making up

Sew a button on the cast-off end to correspond with the buttonhole on the cast-on end. Sew another button in the centre of the front (optional). Weave in all loose ends.

These cuffs are knitted using a simple cable and I have added a pretty border to give them a unique touch.

SCALLOP WRIST WARMERS

Materials:

1 ball of light worsted (DK/8-ply) merino
   yarn in burnt orange; 100g/273yd/250m

Needles:

1 pair of 3.75mm (UK 9, US 5) and 1 pair of
   4.5mm (UK 7, US 7) knitting needles

1 cable needle

Instructions:

Make two.

Using 3.75mm (UK 9, US 5) needles, cast on 39 sts.

Border

Row 1: (RS) *k1, yo, k4, sk2po, k4, yo, k1*, rep from * to * to end of row.

Row 2: *p2 ,k9, p2*, rep from * to * to end of row.

Row 3: *k2, yo, k3, sk2po, k3, yo, k2*, rep from * to * to end of row.

Row 4: *p3, k7, p3*, rep from * to * to end of row.

Row 5: *k3, yo, k2, sk2po, k2, yo, k3*, rep from * to * to end of row.

Row 6: *p4, k5, p4*, rep from * to * to end of row.

Row 7: *k4, yo, k1, sk2po, k1, yo, k4*, rep from * to * to end of row.

Row 8: *p5, k3, p5*, rep from * to * to end of row.

Row 9: *k5, yo, sk2po, yo, k5*, rep from * to * to end of row.

Row 10: Purl.

Change to 4.5mm (UK 7, US 7) needles.

Weave pattern

Row 1: Knit (first time only inc 7 sts evenly across row) (46 sts).

Rows 2, 4 and 6: Purl.

Row 3: *Work right crossover on 4 sts as follows: slip 2 sts onto cable needle and hold at back of work, k2, then k2 from cable needle*, rep from * to * to last 2 sts, k2.

Row 5: k2, *work left crossover on 4 sts as follows: slip 2 sts onto cable needle and hold at front of work, k2, then k2 from cable needle*, rep from * to * to end of row.

Repeat rows 1–6 until work measures 7½in (19cm).

Change to 3.75mm (UK 9/US 5) needles.

Next row: k4, *k2tog, k7*, rep from * to * to the last 6 sts, k2tog, k4.

Cast off all sts.

Making up

With RS facing, use a tapestry needle and mattress stitch to join the side seams 2in (5cm) up from the finger end opening. Leave a gap of 2⅜in (6cm) and then join the seam to the base of the border. This will leave the border open at the wrist end.

Weave in all loose ends.

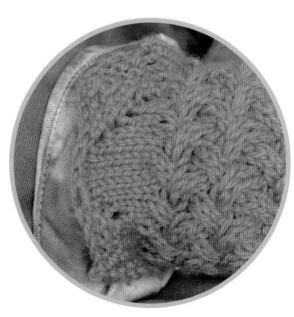

This is a really simple scarf adding a twist to a basic rib. I have added contrasting pompoms to add a bit of fun.

POMPOM SCARF

Materials:

5 balls of light worsted (DK/8-ply) yarn:
  4 x sapphire (A), 1 x parchment (B);
  50g/144yd/132m

2 pieces of card

Tools:

1 pair of 5mm (UK 6, US 8)
  knitting needles

Scissors

Knitting note

Threading a darning needle with the yarn to wind the wool around the cardboard rings makes it much easier.

Instructions:

Initial rows

Rows 1–2: Using 5mm (UK 6, US 8) needles and yarn A cast on 42 sts, ktbl on return row (i.e. row 2).

Scarf pattern

Row 1: (right side) *p3, k3*, repeat from * to * until the end of the row.

Row 2: Knit.

Next rows: Repeat rows 1 and 2 until work measures 67in (170cm).

Cast off sts.

Pompom (make 4)

1 Cut out two identical 1¼in (3.25cm) diameter circles of cardboard.

2 Cut a ½in (1.5cm) diameter round hole in the middle of each circle.

3 Holding the two rings of cardboard together, wind yarn B evenly and tightly round and round, passing each winding through the hole in the middle and over the outer edge of the cardboard ring until the hole is filled with yarn.

4 Carefully cut through the yarn at the outer edge of the rings, making sure that all the yarn remains in place.

5 Take a piece of matching yarn and wind it between the two outer rings. Tie this tightly around the centre of the two rings with two knots to secure.

6 Remove your pompom from the cardboard rings and roll it around in your hands to make it fluffy. Trim the edges to even them out.

Making up

Use a tapestry needle to sew in all ends of wool by weaving them into the sts on the rear of your scarf. Sew a pompom into each corner of your scarf using spare yarn and a tapestry needle.

LONG, COOL BEANIE

Materials:

2 balls of light worsted (DK/8-ply) pure wool yarn in red; 50g/137yd/125m

Needles:

1 pair of 3.25mm (UK 10, US 3) knitting needles

Size:

To fit an average adult head

Gauge (tension)

32 sts and 30 rows to 4in (10cm) measured over single rib (measured without stretching).

Instructions:

Cast on 128 sts.

Row 1: (k1, p1) to end.

Rep row 1 sixty-one times more until work measures approximately 8¼in (21cm).

Row 63: *sl1 knitwise, k2tog, psso, (k1, p1) six times, k1, rep from * seven times more (112 sts).

Row 64 (and every even-numbered row): (k1, p1) to end of row.

Row 65: *sl1 knitwise, k2tog, psso, (k1, p1) five times, k1, rep from * to end (96 sts).

Row 67: *sl1 knitwise, k2tog, psso, (k1, p1) four times, k1, rep from * to end (80 sts).

Row 69: *sl1 knitwise, k2tog, psso, (k1, p1) three times, k1, rep from * to end (64 sts).

Row 71: *sl1 knitwise, k2tog, psso, (k1, p1) twice, k1, rep from * to end (48 sts).

Row 73: *sl1 knitwise, k2tog, psso, k1, p1, k1, rep from * to end (32 sts).

Row 74: (p2tog) sixteen times (16 sts).

Row 75: (k2tog) eight times.

Cut yarn and thread through rem 8 sts.

Making up

Stitch back seam and weave in all loose ends.

Cosy Cool

This hat is ideal for anyone who prefers understated style. The ribbing stretches to accommodate a range of head sizes and the hat is versatile: it can be worn slouchy or rolled up to form a neat brim.

CANDY PINK BOOTEES

Materials:

1 ball of fingering (4-ply) baby yarn in pink, and an
oddment in white; 50g/191yd/175m

20in (50cm) of pretty pink baby ribbon

Needles:

1 pair of 3.75mm (UK 9, US 5) knitting needles

Instructions:

Make two.

Using pink yarn, cast on 37 sts.

Row 1: knit.

Row 2: K1, *inc in next st, K15, inc in next st*,
K1, rep from * to * once more, K1.

Row 3: knit.

Row 4: K2, *inc in next st, K15, inc in next st*,
K3, rep from * to * once, K2.

Row 5: knit.

Row 6: K3, *inc in next st, K15, inc in next st*,
K5, rep from * to * once, K3.

Row 7: knit.

Row 8: K4, *inc in next st, K15, inc in next st*,
K7, rep from * to * once, K4.

Row 9: knit.

Row 10: K5, *inc in next st, K15, inc in next st*,
K9, rep from * to * once, K5.

Row 11: knit.

Join in white and work in two-colour pattern
as follows:

Row 12: knit in pink.

Row 13: purl in pink.

Row 14: using white K1, *sl1, K1*, rep from *
to * to end of row.

Row 15: rep row 14.

Row 16: knit in white.

Row 17: purl in white.

Row 18: using pink, K2, *sl1, K1*, rep from
* to * to last 2 sts, K2.

Row 19: using pink, P1, K1, *sl1, K1*, rep from
* to * to last st, P1.

Rows 20–27: rep rows 12 to 19.

Rows 28–29: GS in white.

Break white and continue in pink :

Row 30: K33, sl1, K1, psso, turn.

Row 31: sl1, K9, P2tog, turn.

Row 32: sl1, K9, sl1, K1, psso, turn.

Rows 33–48: rep rows 31 and 32 eight times.

Row 49: rep row 31.

Row 50: knit.

Rows 51–53: GS.

Make eyelet holes as follows.

Row 54: K1, *yfwd, K2tog*, rep from * to * to
end of row.

Rows 55–57: GS, decreasing 1 st in centre of
last row.

Work 20 rows in K2, P2 rib.

Cast off in rib.

Making up

Sew up the foot and back seams neatly. Turn
over the ribbed top to form a cuff. Cut the
ribbon in half and thread one half through the
holes at the ankle of each bootee using a large-
eyed, blunt-ended needle. Tie in a pretty bow.

Penguins are always fun to work with and these cuffs will liven up any boots. This pattern is suitable for a knitter who has mastered the basics. To change the look, try knitting them in different colours.

PENGUIN BOOT CUFFS

Materials:

2 balls each of DK (8-ply) pure alpaca yarn in pale turquoise (A) and 1 ball each in gold (B), mid-blue (C) and cream (D); 50g/109yd/100m

Needles:

1 pair of 5mm (UK 6, US 8) knitting needles

Instructions:

Make two.

Cast on 58sts in yarn A.

Knit into the back of the sts to form a neat edge.

Using the chart place pattern as follows:

Even row numbers are knit and odd numbers are purl.

Row 1: k2A, *3B, 2A, 3B, 6A* rep from * to * three times more.

Continue working from the chart until row 18. Cut off yarn C. The rest of the knitting is done in yarn A.

Row 19: knit.

Row 20: purl.

Now continue in ribbing.

Ribbing

Row 1: *k2, p2* rep until the last two sts, k2.

Row 2: *p2, k2* rep until the last two sts, p2.

Rows 3–20: Rep rows 1 and 2 nine more times.

Row 21: As row 1.

Row 22: Cast off sts.

Making up

Use a tapestry needle to sew in loose ends by weaving them into stitches at the back of your work.

With right side facing, use a mattress stitch to join the side seams of the pattern component of the boot cuff.

Sew up the rib on the rear side of the boot cuff.

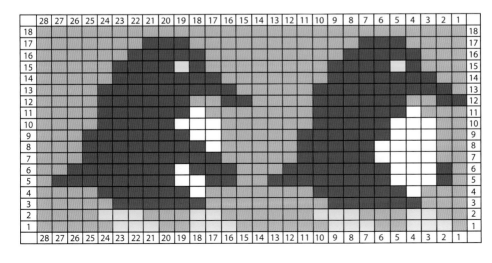

Dot to Dot
Attach the spots in whatever arrangement you want – you could even create more than six if you like.

LADYBUG TEA COSY

Gauge (tension)
5 sts = 1in (2.5cm).

Instructions:

Make two.

Using black yarn and 4mm (UK 8, US 6) needles, cast on 42 sts.

Work 14 rows in SS.

Change to red yarn and knit until work measures 16.5cm (6½in) from the cast-on edge.

Shape the top

Row 1: change to black yarn and k7, k2tog, *k6, k2tog*, rep from * to * to last st, k1.

Row 2: purl.

Row 3: k6, k2tog, *k5, k2tog*, rep from * to * to last st, k1.

Row 4: purl.

Row 5: k5, k2tog, *k4, k2tog*, rep from * to * to last st, k1.

Row 6: purl.

Row 7: k4, k2tog, *k3, k2tog*, rep from * to * to last st, k1.

Row 8: purl.

Row 9: k3, k2tog, *k2, k2tog*, rep from * to * to last st, k1.

Row 10: purl.

Row 11: k2, k2tog, *k1, k2tog*, rep from * to * to last st, k1.

Row 12: purl.

Row 13: k1, k2tog, *k2tog*, rep from * to * to last st, k1.

Cut yarn and place sts on stitch holder.

Making up

Place the wrong sides of the cosy together (right sides facing out). Thread a tapestry needle with the black tail on the back stitch holder. Graft the sts on the stitch holders together.

Sew the top

Continue sewing down one side for 7.5cm (3in).

Fasten off and hide tail in the seam.

Repeat on other side of cosy.

Sew the bottom

Thread a tapestry needle with one of the black tails of yarn from the cast on edge.

Sew up one side for 4cm (1½in).

Fasten off and hide tail in the seam.

Repeat on the other side of cosy.

Wing division

Using black yarn and stem stitch, embroider the wing division up the centre of the cosy.

Spots (make 6)

Using black yarn and 4.5mm (UK 7, US 7) DPN, cast on 3 sts.

Row 1: kfb in each st.

Row 2: knit.

Row 3: k2tog across row.

Row 4: sk2po.

Cut yarn and pull through rem sts.

Using a tapestry needle and tails, sew spots on cosy.

Antennae (make 2)

Measure 1in (2.5cm) from centre top of cosy.

Using black yarn and 4.5mm (UK 7, US 7) DPN, pick up and knit 4 sts.

Row 1: k4; do not turn but slide sts to other end of needle.

Repeat this row until work measures 2½in (6cm).

Next row: kfb, k2, kfb, (6 sts); do not turn but slide sts to other end of needle.

Work two more rows even with these 6 sts.

Cut yarn leaving a 15cm (6in) tail.

With a tapestry needle pull tail across the back and through the 6 sts. Pull the tail down through the centre of the cord – pull it tight enough that the antenna stands upright. Secure tail underneath the cosy. Repeat for the other antenna.

Materials:
1 ball each of worsted (aran/10-ply) yarn in black and red; 50g/93yd/85m

Tools:
1 pair of 4mm (UK 8, US 6) knitting needles and 1 pair of 4.5mm (UK 7, US 7) DPN
2 stitch holders

MINI RUDOLPH

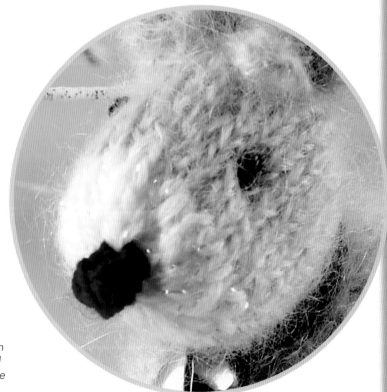

Frosty the Red-Nosed Reindeer
*This alternative reindeer is made from
pale grey, blue, sparkly white and red
yarn, a very magical companion to the
more natural-coloured Rudolph.*

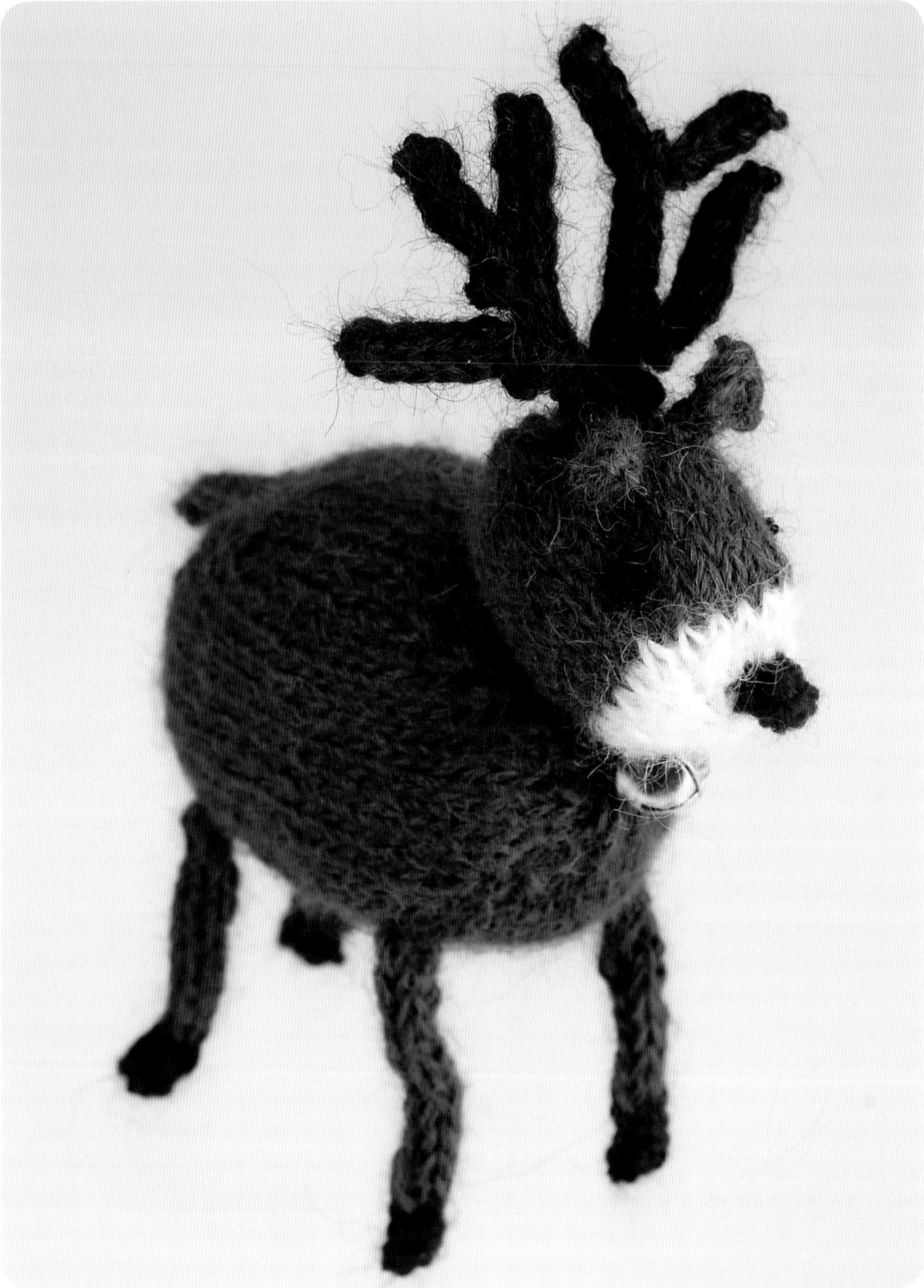

Instructions:

Body

Using brown yarn, cast on 14 sts, P 1 row.

Work inc rows as follows:

K1, (K1fb, K1, K1fb) to last st, K1. P 1 row (22 sts).

K1, (K1fb, K3, K1fb) to last st, K1. P 1 row (30 sts).

K1, (K1fb, K5, K1fb) to last st, K1. P 1 row (38 sts).

K1, (K1fb, K7, K1fb) to last st, K1. P 1 row (46 sts).

K1, (K1fb, K9, K1fb) to last st, K1. P 1 row (54 sts).

Work 10 rows in SS.

Work dec rows as follows:

K1, (K2tog, K9, ssk) to last st, K1. P 1 row (46 sts).

K1, (K2tog, K7, ssk) to last st, K1. P 1 row (38 sts).

K1, (K2tog, K5, ssk) to last st, K1. P 1 row (30 sts).

K1, (K2tog, K3, ssk) to last st, K1. P 1 row (22 sts).

K1, (K2tog, K1, ssk) to last st, K1. P 1 row (14 sts).

Thread yarn through rem sts, fasten off.

Head

Using brown yarn, cast on 14 sts, P 1 row.

Work inc rows as follows:

K1, (K1fb, K1, K1fb) to last st, K1. P 1 row (22 sts).

K1, (K1fb, K3, K1fb) to last st, K1. P 1 row (30 sts).

Work 8 rows in SS.

Change to cream fingering (4-ply) and work dec rows as follows:

K1, (K2tog, K3, ssk) to last st, K1. P 1 row (22 sts).

K1, (K2tog, K1, ssk) to last st, K1. P 1 row (14 sts).

Thread yarn through rem sts. Fasten off.

Bobble (nose)

Using red yarn, cast on 1 st.

Next row: knit into the front, back and front of the st (3 sts).

Starting with a K row, work 3 rows in SS.

Next row: sl1, K2tog, psso (1 st). Run a length of yarn around the edges of the bobble, leaving a tail to attach to the head.

Antlers (make 2)

Using dark brown yarn, cast on 3 sts and work an i-cord $1\frac{5}{8}$in (4cm) long (see page 18). Thread yarn through sts and fasten off. Make two more i-cords in this way, one 1in (2.5cm) long and another $\frac{5}{8}$in (1.5cm) long.

Legs (make 4)

Using black yarn, cast on 4 sts and work 2 rows using the i-cord technique. Change to MC and continue until the leg measures $1\frac{5}{8}$in (4cm). Thread yarn through sts and fasten off.

Ears (make 2)

Using brown yarn, cast on 3 sts, starting with a K row, work 4 rows in SS.

Next row: sl1, K2tog, psso.

Fasten off rem st.

Tail

Using MC, cast on 7 sts, cast off.

Collar

Using the 2.75mm crochet hook, work a chain long enough to go around the reindeer's neck. Fasten off. Alternatively, braid a length of yarn to make the collar.

Making up

Sew the head and body seams, stuffing as you close. Attach the head to the body, using the picture as a guide. Attach the legs, tail and ears. To make the antlers, sew the shorter i-cords to the longer i-cord. Sew in the ends. Sew the antlers to the head, behind the ears. Sew the bobble to the centre of head for the nose. Using black yarn, embroider the eyes. Sew the collar in place and attach the bell.

TULIP

Instructions:

Petal (make 3)

With orange yarn and 3.25mm (UK 10; US 3) needles,
cast on 5 sts.

Round 1: k.

Row 1: k each st tbl.

Row 2: k1, inc 1, k1, inc 1, k1 (7 sts).

Row 3: k.

Row 4: k2, inc 1, k1, inc 1, k2 (9 sts).

Row 5: k.

Row 6: k3, inc 1, k1, inc 1, k3 (11 sts).

Row 7: k.

Row 8: k4, inc 1, k1, inc 1, k4 (13 sts).

Row 9: k.

Row 10: k5, inc 1, k1, inc 1, k5 (15 sts).

Knit 8 rows.

Row 19: sl 1, k1, psso, k11, k2tog (13 sts).

Row 20: k.

Row 21: sl 1, k1, psso, k9, k2tog (11 sts).

Row 22: k.

Row 23: sl 1, k1, psso, k7, k2tog (9 sts).

Row 24: k.

Row 25: sl 1, k1, psso, k5, k2tog (7 sts).

Row 26: k.

Row 27: sl 1, k1, psso, k3, k2tog (5 sts).

Row 28: k.

Row 29: sl 1, k1, psso, k1, k2tog (3 sts).

Row 30: sl 1, k2tog, psso; fasten off.

Stalk

With green yarn and two double-pointed needles, cast
on 5 sts.

Row 1: k5; do not turn but slide sts to other end
of needle.

Rep this row until work measures 21cm (8¼in);
fasten off.

Making up

Fold over ¼in (5mm) at either end of one of the pipe
cleaners and slip it inside the stalk. Stitch the ends of
the stalk closed. Stitch the top of the stalk to the base of
one of the petals. Cut the second pipe cleaner into three
equal lengths, fold each one in half and attach to the top
of the stalk to create stamens. Wrap the two remaining
petals around the first and stitch.

EMILY KNITTING BEAR

Materials:

1 ball each of light worsted (DK/8-ply) yarn in brown, pale green and white, plus oddments in green, pink and yellow; 50g/137yd/125m

Small amount of toy stuffing

2 x 6mm round black beads for eyes

Black embroidery thread or floss for features

2 tiny pearl, heart-shaped buttons

Cocktail stick

2 small cotton balls for slippers

Fuse wire for glasses

2 small white beads for ends of knitting needles

All-purpose glue

Tools:

1 pair of 3.25mm (UK 10, US 3) knitting needles

Sewing needle

Stitch holder

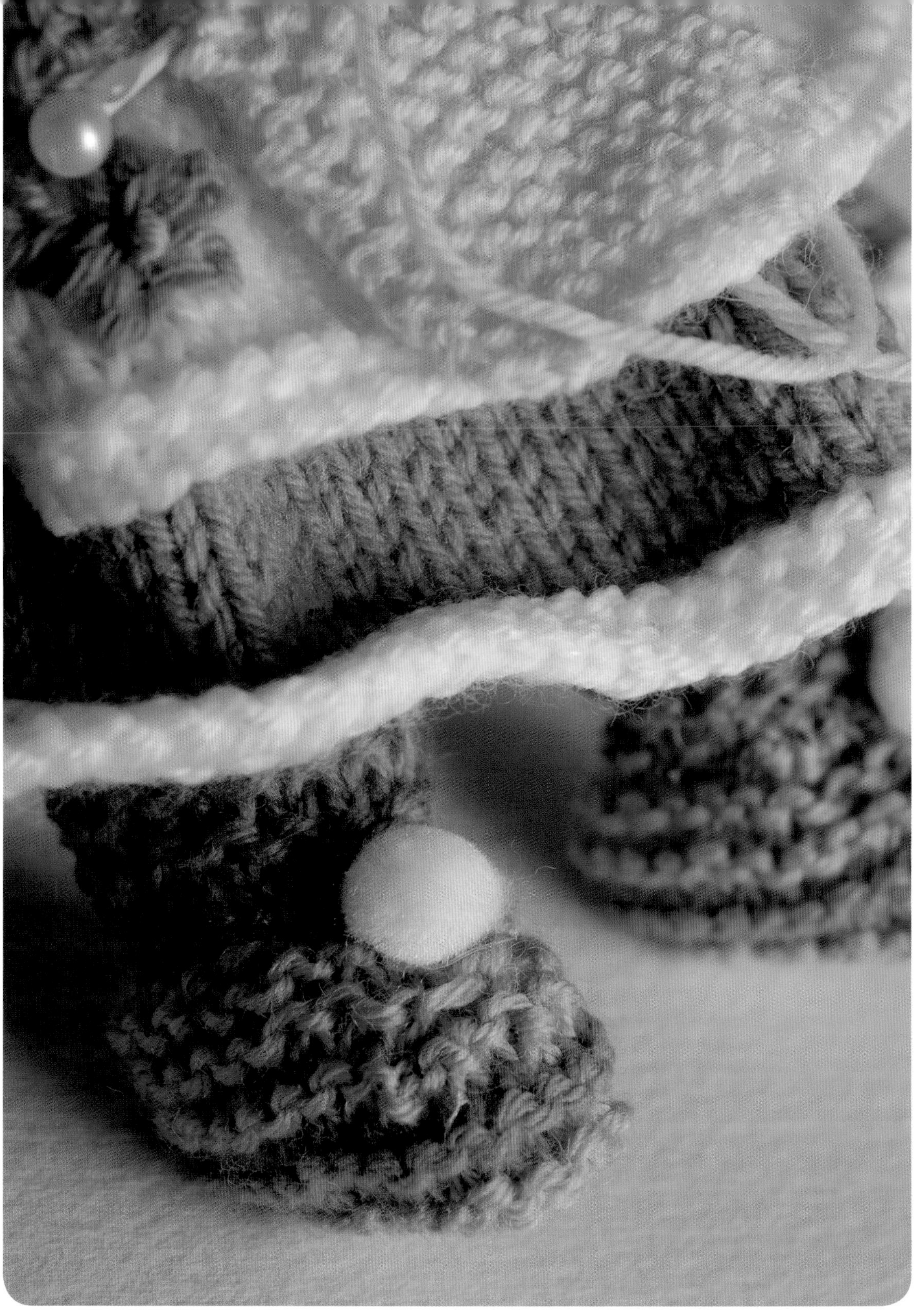

Instructions:

Make the bear in brown yarn following the instructions on page 41.

Dress

Back and front (both worked the same):

Using pale green, cast on 24 sts.

Rows 1–4: SS.

Rows 5–6: cast off 2 sts at beg of each row (20 sts).

Rows 7–8: SS.

Row 9: K2tog, knit to last 2 sts, K2tog.

Row 10: purl.

Rows 11–16: SS.

Rows 17–18: change to white and GS.

Cast off.

Using pale green, work skirt as follows:

With RS facing, pick up and knit 24 sts along cast-on edge of dress front.
Next row: purl.
Next row: knit twice into each st (48 sts).
Continue in SS and complete as given in pattern.
Repeat the above, on dress back.
When work measures 2¾in (7cm) change to white and work 2 rows GS.

Cast off.

Apron

Using white, cast on 36 sts.

Rows 1–4: GS.

Row 5: knit.

Row 6: K3, purl to last 3 sts, K3.

Rows 7–16: repeat rows 5 and 6, five times.

Row 17: (K3, K2tog) to last 3 sts, K3 (21 sts).

Row 18: cast on 18 sts, knit to end.

Row 19: cast on 18 sts, knit to end.

Row 20: knit across all sts.

Cast off.

Work in all the yarn ends. Embroider a small flower and leaf on to one corner of the apron using pink and green.

Slippers

Using pale green, cast on 14 sts.

Row 1: knit.

Row 2: inc in each st to end (28 sts).

Continue in GS.

Rows 3–4: knit using green.

Rows 5–6: knit using pink.

Row 7: knit using green.

Next row: K2tog, K8, (K2tog) four times, K8, K2tog.

Next row: K9, (K2tog) twice, K9.

Next row: knit.

Cast off. Stitch the seam along the base and back of the shoe.

Glasses

Take a short length of fuse wire and twist it around a pencil to give two small circles. Arrange them into a pleasing shape, making sure they fit over the bear's eyes. Use the photograph for guidance. Bend each end of the wire to form the arms and push them into the bear's head on each side of the eyes. Secure with a few stitches.

Knitting

Cast on 10 sts and work 18 rows GS. Do not cast off.

Making up

Lightly stuff the slippers, place the base of the bear's leg inside the shoe and stitch it in place. Sew a cotton ball to the front of each slipper. Sew the side seams on the dress, slip it on to the bear and sew the shoulder seams. Sew the two heart buttons on the front. Tie the apron around the bear's waist and secure the ties with a few stitches. Make knitting needles by breaking a cocktail stick in half and gluing a bead on to the broken end of each one. Slip the knitting on to both tiny needles, and secure the needles on to the bear's paws with a dab of glue.

SIDEWAYS PHONE SOCK

Materials:

- 1 ball of light worsted (DK/8-ply) yarn in lilac (A); 50g/137yd/125m
- 1 ball of light worsted (DK/8-ply) chenille yarn in white (B); 50g/120yd/110m

Tools:

- 1 pair of 4.5mm (UK 7, US 7) knitting needles
- Sewing needle
- Scissors
- Tape measure

Knitting note

When using two colours, twist yarns up the side of the work as you go. This keeps a neater edge.

Instructions:

Increasing

Row 1: Using 4.5mm (UK 7, US 7) knitting needles, make a loop with yarn A.

Rows 2–3: Working in garter stitch, inc 1 st beg of every row until you have 5 sts.

Rows 4–5: Join in colour B and knit, increasing as before until you have 9 sts.

Rows 6–7: Using colour A, continue increasing until you have 13 sts.

Rows 8–9: Using colour B, continue increasing until you have 17 sts.

Next rows: Continue in this manner, increasing and alternating colours until you have 34 sts.

Decreasing

Next rows: Keeping to the same pattern of alternating colours as above, start decreasing 1 st at beg of every row until you have 2 sts rem.

Next row: k2tog.

Fasten off.

Making up

Close the side and bottom seams with mattress stitch.

This simple phone sock makes a soft cosy for your mobile phone and is knitted in garter stitch so it is great for the beginner.

LADY'S SMOCK MUG HUG

Materials:

- 1 ball of light worsted (DK/8-ply) yarn in pink
- 20 x gold-coloured glass beads
- 1 fancy pink button

Needles:

1 pair of 3.75mm (UK 9, US 5) knitting needles

Blunt-ended sewing needle for smocking

Size:

9 x 3¼in (23 x 8cm)

Instructions:

Cast on 11 sts.

Knit 2 rows.

Continue in GS.

Inc 1 st at each end of next and every alt row until 23 sts on needle.

Proceed in pattern as follows:

Row 1: (RS facing) K2 ,(P3, K1) four times, P3, K2.

Row 2: K2, (K3, P1) four times, K3, K2.

Rep rows 1 and 2 until work measures 7in (18cm), ending on row 2.

Change to GS and shape the button edge as follows:

Dec 1 st at each end of next and every alt row until 17 sts rem.

Next row: to make buttonhole, K2tog, K6, yrn, K2tog, knit to last 2 sts, K2tog.

Next row: knit, knitting into the yrn of the previous row.

Continue shaping as before until 11 sts rem.

Knit 2 rows.

Cast off.

Making up and smocking

Work in all ends neatly. You will need to count your rows and divide them equally into sections. There should be five diamond shapes going down the centre of the design and six on either side. With RS facing and using a blunt-ended needle and pink yarn, catch together the lines of knit stitches to form the diamond shapes. Begin at the top of the piece of work and draw together the stitches in the two left-hand lines first, then those in the two right-hand lines, and finally the two inner lines. Stitch a bead on to each intersection. Follow the picture for guidance. Sew on the pink button to correspond with the buttonhole.

Give traditional English afternoon tea a contemporary twist with these pretty mug hugs, knitted in any colours you choose.

ANGEL CAKE

Instructions:

Sides of cake

Cast on 60 sts in pink yarn. Work in g st.

Rows 1–5: knit.

Rows 6–7: change to pale pink and work in st st, starting with a K row.

Rows 8–9: change back to pink and continue in st st.

Rows 10–11: change to pale pink and continue in st st.

Rows 12–13: change to pink and continue in st st.

Rows 14–15: change to pale pink and continue in st st.

Rows 16–21: change to pink and work in g st.

Cast off.

Top and bottom of cake

Cast on 14 sts.
Rows 1–21: st st.
Cast off.

Flower

Cast on 8 sts using pink. Work in st st.

Row 1: knit.

Row 2: purl.

Row 3: knit, increasing every st (16 sts).

Row 4: purl.

Row 5: knit, increasing every st (32 sts).

Row 6: purl.

Row 7: knit, increasing every st (64 sts).

Row 8: purl.

Row 9: knit, increasing every fourth st across row (80 sts).

Cast off.

Materials:

1 ball each of fingering (4-ply) yarn in pink and pale pink

Oddment of green yarn

Cardboard for insert, 2¼ x 7¾in (6 x 20cm)

Toy stuffing

Needles:

1 pair of 3.25mm (UK 10, US 3) knitting needles

153

Leaves

Cast on 2 sts and work in g st.

Row 1: knit.

Row 2: * inc every st * (4 sts).

Rows 3–4: knit.

Row 5: repeat from * to * (6 sts).

Rows 6–7: knit.

Row 8: K2tog at beg and end of row (4 sts).

Rows 9–10: knit.

Row 11: K2tog, K2tog (2 sts).

Row 12: K2tog.

Break yarn and pull through last stitch.

Making up

Join together the two short edges of the cake side to make a tube. Working on the right side of the knitting, use small running stitches to attach the cake base to the side – working on the right side will make a ridge on the edge of the cake. Roll the cardboard into a flattened tube shape, overlapping the ends, insert it into the cake and stuff. Sew the top on the cake in the same way as the base. Roll the flower up into a pleasing shape and secure it with a few stitches. Attach the flower and the leaves to the top of the cake.

This delicious chocolate version of the angel cake is made using dark brown and cream fingering (4-ply) wool.

JORNA ALIEN

Materials:

1 ball each of light worsted (DK/8-ply) yarn in variegated purple and lilac; 50g/137yd/125m

1 ball of light worsted (DK/8-ply) multicoloured fluffy yarn; 100g/106yd/97m

Small amounts of red yarn for mouth and aqua yarn for antennae

2 beads for eyes

Toy stuffing

Black thread

Tools:

1 pair 3mm (UK 11, US 2) knitting needles

Sewing needle

3mm (US D-0, UK 11) crochet hook

Instructions:

Body (make 1)

Cast on 10 sts in variegated purple.

Row 1: inc each st (20 sts).

Row 2: purl.

Row 3: *k1, inc 1* rep from * to * to end (30 sts).

Row 4: purl.

Row 5: k12, k inc in each of next 6 st, k12 (36 sts).

Rows 6–18: st st.

Row 19: k12, k2tog six times, k12 (30 sts).

Row 20: purl.

Row 21: *k1, k2tog* rep from * to * to end (20 sts).

Rows 22–30: st st.

Row 31: k2tog row (10 sts).

Row 32: purl.

Row 33: k2tog row (5 sts).

Row 34: purl and cast off.

The fun-loving Jorna aliens are short and squat with friendly faces.

Ears (make 2)

Cast on 4 sts in lilac.

Rows 1–2: st st.

Row 3: k2tog (2 sts).

Row 4: p2tog. Cast off.

Face (make 1)

Cast on 2 sts in lilac.

Row 1: inc each st (4 sts).

Row 2: purl.

Rows 3–4: rep rows 1 and 2 once (8 sts).

Row 5: purl.

Row 6: k3, inc next 2 k3 (10 sts).

Row 7: purl.

Row 8: k3, k inc next 4, k3 (14 sts).

Row 9: purl.

Row 10: k3, inc next 8, k3 (22 sts).

Rows 11–13: st st.

Row 14: k2tog each end (20 sts).

Row 15: purl.

Row 16: k2tog, k3, k2tog five times, k3, k2tog (13 sts).

Row 17: purl.

Row 18: k2tog three times, k1, k2tog three times (7 sts).

Row 19: purl.

Row 20: k2tog, k3, k2tog (5 sts).

Row 21: p2tog, p1, p2tog (3 sts). Cast off.

Making up

Sew up the back up the centre seam, leaving a small opening. Stuff the alien through this opening, then stitch shut. Pin face on to front of body and stitch on, stuffing as you go. Needlesculpt the nose, then sew on beads for eyes. Embroider a simple mouth, then sew on the ears. Finally, make two antennae as follows:

With a 3mm (US D-0, UK 11) crochet hook and acqua yarn, crochet 7 chains and cut a long thread. Thread this on to a tapestry needle and weave back through the crocheted chain. Stitch in place as shown on either side of the head and fasten off.

MUSHROOM

Materials:

- 1 ball each of light worsted (DK/8-ply) wool or wool blend yarn in ivory and dark beige; 50g/137yd/125m
- Toy stuffing

Needles:

Set of four 3mm (UK 11, US 2) DPN

Size:

Approx. 3in (7.5cm) across and 2¾in (7cm) high, including the stalk.

Instructions:

Cap, gills and stalk (in one piece)

With set of four 3.00mm (UK 11; US 2) double-pointed needles and ivory yarn, cast on 12 sts and divide equally between three needles.

Rounds 1–10: k; cut yarn and continue in dark beige yarn.

Round 11: (k1, inc1) six times (18 sts).

Round 12: (k2, inc1) six times (24 sts).

Round 13: (k3, inc1) six times (30 sts).

Round 14: (k4, inc1) six times (36 sts).

Round 15: (k5, inc1) six times (42 sts).

Round 16: (k6, inc1) six times (48 sts); cut yarn and change to ivory.

Rounds 17 and 18: k.

Round 19: (k7, inc1) six times (54 sts).

Round 20: (k8, inc1) six times (60 sts).

Rounds 21–25: k.

Round 26: (k8, k2tog) six times (54 sts).

Round 27 and every odd-numbered round: k.

Round 28: (k7, k2tog) six times (48 sts).

Round 30: (k6, k2tog) six times (42 sts).

Round 32: (k5, k2tog) six times (36 sts).

Round 34: (k4, k2tog) six times (30 sts).

Round 36: (k3, k2tog) six times (24 sts).

Round 38: (k2, k2tog) six times (18 sts).

Round 40: (k1, k2tog) six times (12 sts).

Round 41: (k2tog) six times.

Break yarn and thread through rem 6 sts.

Making up

Stuff the mushroom fairly firmly. Using the yarn ends, oversew the join where the colour change occurs between the gills and the cap. Weave the yarn in and out of the stitches where the top of the stalk meets the gills and pull it up to tighten. The finished mushroom measures approximately 3in (7.5cm) and 2¾in (7cm) high, including the stalk.

Forest Fungi

The main mushroom is made in stocking stitch. Knit the stalk or gills in reverse stocking stitch for a subtle variation in texture, or knit the entire mushroom in a single colour.

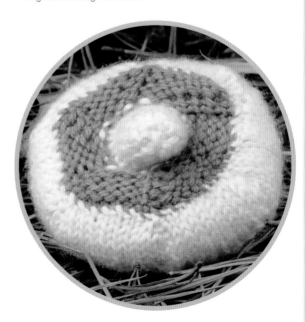

CHERRIES

Materials:

- 1 ball of fingering (4-ply) yarn in red and a small amount in green; 50g/191yd/175m
- Toy stuffing

Tools:

- 1 pair of 2.25mm (UK 13, US 1) knitting needles and 1 pair of 2.25mm (UK 13, US 1) DPN
- Stitch holder

Size:

Approx. 1in (2.5cm) in diameter

Instructions:

Cherry (make 2)

With size 2.25mm (UK 13, US 1) DPN and red yarn, cast on 3 sts.

Row 1 and all odd-numbered (WS) rows until row 19: p to end.

Row 2: inc1 in each st (6 sts).

Row 4: inc1 in each st (12 sts).

Row 6: (k1, inc1) six times (18 sts).

Row 8: (k2, inc1) six times (24 sts).

Rows 9 –13: Beg with a purl row, work in st st (1 row p, 1 row k).

Row 14: (k2, k2tog) six times (18 sts).

Row 16: (k1, k2tog) six times (12 sts).

Row 18: (k2tog) six times (6 sts).

Row 19: (p2tog) three times.

Break yarn, leaving a tail, and thread through rem 3 sts.

Stalk

**With 2.25mm (UK 13; US 1) double-pointed needles and green yarn, cast on 2 sts.

Row 1: k2; do not turn but slide sts to other end of needle.

Rows 2–18: Rep row 1 seventeen times more; do not fasten off**.

Leave sts on a stitch holder or spare needle and make a second stalk by repeating instructions from ** to **.

Slip sts on holder back on to needle (4 sts), knit across all sts, then cast off and cut yarn, leaving a tail.

Making up

On each cherry, pull up the tail of yarn to close the stitches on the last row, then thread the yarn on to a tapestry needle. Stitch the side seam using a grafting technique, adding stuffing before reaching the end of the seam. Insert the end of the stalk into the gap on the cast-on edge, then run the end of the yarn through all the stitches on the cast-on edge and pull up to close. Using the tail of yarn at the top of the stalk, oversew the cast-off row and pull up firmly before fastening off.

Cheery Cherry

Cherries can be made into pies, soup or even wine; but these knitted versions are best kept as decorations! You could attach a brooch back to the stalk and wear the cherry as a delightful accessory.

RED ROBIN HEADBAND

Materials:

1 ball of worsted (aran/10-ply) Bluefaced Leicester yarn in red;
    50g/91yd/83m

Needles:

1 pair of 5mm (UK 6, US 8) knitting needles

1 cable needle

Instructions:

Cast on 87 sts, then ktbl to form a neat edge.

Row 1: k1, p2tog, *k1, p1, rep from * to last 3 sts, p2tog, k1 (85 sts).

Row 2: * k1, p1, rep from * to end.

Insert pattern as follows (the pattern is repeated five times across each row as a 17-st pattern repeat):

Row 1 (RS): * p6, k2tog, yfrn, p1, yo, sl1, k1, psso, p6, rep from * to end.

Row 2: *k6, p1, k3, p1, k6, rep from * to end.

Row 3: *p5, k2tog, yfrn, p3, yo, sl1, k1, psso, p5, rep from * to end.

Row 4: *(k5, p1) twice, k5, rep from * to end.

Row 5: *p4, k2tog, yfrn, (p1, k1) twice, p1, yo, sl1, k1, psso, p4, rep from * to end.

Row 6: *k4, p1, k2, p1, k1, p1, k2, p1, k4, rep from * to end.

Row 7: *p3, k2tog, yfrn, p2, k1, p1, k1, p2, yo, sl1, k1, psso, p3, rep from * to end.

Row 8: *(k3, p1) twice, k1, (p1, k3) twice, rep from * to end.

Row 9: *p2, k2tog, yfrn, p2, k2tog, yfrn, p1, yo, sl1, k1, psso, p2, yo, sl1, k1, psso, p2, rep from * to end.

Row 10: *k2, (p1, k3) three times, p1, k2, rep from * to end.

Row 11 (Bobble row): *p2, (k1, p1, k1, p1) into next st,

turn, p4, turn, k4, turn, p4, turn, sl1, k1, psso, k2tog, turn, p2tog, turn, slip bobble onto right-hand needle (bobble completed), p2, k2tog, yfrn, p3, yo, sl1, k1, psso, p2, make second bobble and slip it onto right-hand needle, p2, rep from * to end.

Row 12: As row 4.

Row 13: k1, p2tog, *k1, p1, rep from * to last 3 sts, k2tog, p1 (83 sts).

Row 14: *k1, p1, rep from * to end.

Cast off all sts.

Making up

With RS facing, join seams together using mattress stitch. Weave in all loose ends.

This headband combines lace with bobbles. It is knitted in bright red to give it a festive feel.

Everyone loves snowmen. I have knitted the motif using intarsia to avoid large loops at the back of the work, and cut-off lengths of white and black yarn to make the knitting easier.

FROSTY
WRIST WARMERS

Materials:

3 balls of light worsted (DK/8-ply) merino yarn
– 1 x red (A), 1 x white (B), 1 x black (C):
100g/273yd/250m

Needles:

1 pair of 4mm (UK 8, US 6)
knitting needles

Instructions:

Make two.

The black yarn is used double throughout to accentuate the snowman's hat and buttons.

Using yarn A, cast on 40 sts, then ktbl to form a neat edge.

Rows 1–16: *k1, p1*, rep from * to * to end of row.

Rows 17–18: st st.

Row 19: k2A, *k1B, k4A*, rep from * to * to last pattern rep, k2A.

Row 20: p1A, *p3B, p2A*, rep from * to * to last pattern rep, p1A.

Row 21: *k2B, k1A, k2B*, rep from * to * to end of row.

Row 22: As row 20.

Row 23: As row 19. Cut off yarn B.

Rows 24–26: st st in yarn A.

Row 27: Work row 1 of the chart, placing the 2 snowmen motifs as follows: k7A, k7B, k12A, k7B, k7A to set the spacing, then continue to work rows 2–26 from chart. Cut off yarns B and C.

Next 2 rows: st st, using yarn A.

Next 2 rows: *k1, p1*, rep to end of row.

Cast off all sts.

Making up

With RS facing, use a tapestry needle and mattress stitch to join the side seams, 4in (10cm) from the wrist end and 2in (5cm) from the finger end. This will leave a gap for your thumb to go through.

Weave in all loose ends.

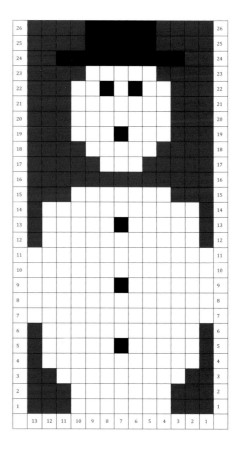

AUTUMN HAZE SCARF

Materials:

3 balls of light worsted (DK/8-ply) silk blend yarn in variegated fawn/grey; 100g/295yd/270m

Needles:

1 pair of 7mm (UK 2, US 10½) knitting needles

Instructions:

Use the yarns tripled throughout the pattern.

Initial rows

Rows 1–2: cast on 16 sts, then ktbl on return row (i.e. row 2).

Scarf pattern

Rows 1 and 2: *k2, p2*, rep to end.

Rows 3 and 4: *p2, k2*, rep to end.

Repeat rows 1–4 until work measures approximately 61½in (156cm).

Cast off sts.

Weave in all loose ends using a tapestry needle.

This is a really simple scarf that is made in variegated wool used tripled, which adds texture to the stitch. The scarf uses a simple moss stitch knitted on large needles.

Blooming Lovely!
The directions opposite are for an adult-size hat. To make a child-size version, follow the same pattern but use fingering (4-ply) yarn and 3mm (UK 11, US 3) knitting needles.

Materials:
2 balls of light worsted (DK/8-ply) pure wool or wool blend yarn in damson, and small amounts in dusty pink and apricot; 50g/137yd/125m
2 x 1¼in (29mm) buttons
Toy stuffing

Needles:
3.75mm (UK 9, US 5) knitting needles

Sizes:
To fit an average female adult head

FLOWER POWER BEANIE

Gauge (tension)
15 sts and 25 rows to 4in (10cm) measured over single rib, using 3.75mm (UK 9, US 5) knitting needles (measured without stretching).

Instructions:
Using damson yarn, cast on 112 sts.

Row 1: (k1, p1) to end.

Rep row 1 thirty-five times more.

Row 37: *sl1 knitwise, k2tog, psso, (k1, p1) five times, k1, rep from * to end (96 sts).

Row 38 (and every even-numbered row): (k1, p1) to end of row.

Row 39: *sl1 knitwise, k2tog, psso, (k1, p1) four times, k1, rep from * to end (80 sts).

Row 41: *sl1 knitwise, k2tog, psso, (k1, p1) three times, k1, rep from * to end (64 sts).

Row 43: *sl1 knitwise, k2tog, psso, (k1, p1) twice, k1, rep from * to end (48 sts).

Row 45: *sl1 knitwise, k2tog, psso, k1, p1, k1, rep from * to end (32 sts).

Row 47: (k2tog) sixteen times (16 sts).

Row 49: (k2tog) eight times.

Cut yarn and thread through rem 8 sts.

Pink Flower
Petals (made in one piece)
Using dusky pink yarn, cast on 11 sts.

Row 1: knit 1 row tbl.

Row 2: k to end.

Row 3: inc 1, k to end (12 sts).

Knit 3 rows.

Row 7: k2tog, k to end (11 sts).

Row 8: k to end.

Row 9: cast off 9, k rem st.

Row 10: k2, cast on 9 (11 sts).

Rep rows 1 to 10 four times, then rows 1 to 8 once; cast off.

Centre
Using apricot yarn, cast on 2 sts.

Row 1: inc1, k to end.

Rep row 1 until there are 6 sts.

Knit 3 rows.

Next row: cast off 1, k to end.

Rep last row until there are 2 sts.

Cast off; break yarn and fasten off.

Make a second flower, reversing the colours.

Making up
Pull up the tail of yarn to gather the stitches on the final row and secure then, with right sides together and using the tail of yarn, stitch the back seam.

To make each flower, bring the two edges of the petals together to make a circle of petals and stitch the lower corners of the two ends together; run a gathering stitch around the centre, along the base of each petal and pull it up tightly to gather. Run a gathering stitch around the edge of the centre, place a tiny wad of polyester stuffing inside and a 1¼in (29mm) button on top of the stuffing, then pull it tightly to gather up and enclose the button. Stitch the flower centre firmly in place in the centre of the petals, then stitch it in place on the hat.

DUCKLING BOOTEES

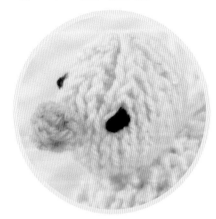

Instructions:

Make two.

Using yellow yarn, cast on 48 sts.

Row 1: knit.

Row 2: (K2, m1, K1) twice, k to last 6 sts, (K1, m1, K2) twice.

Row 3: knit.

Rows 4–5: rep rows 2 and 3 (56 sts).

Rows 6–7: knit.

Row 8: K25, (K1, m1) six times, k to end of row (62 sts).

Work pattern as follows:

Row 9: (RS facing) (K1, P1) to end of row.

Row 10: knit.

Rows 11–24: rep rows 9 and 10 seven times.

Shape foot as follows:

Row 25: K19, (K2tog) twelve times, k to end of row (52 sts).

Row 26: K33, turn.

Row 27: (K2tog) 8 times, K1, turn.

Row 28: K10, turn.

Row 29: (K2tog) 5 times, K3, turn.

Cast off 11 sts, knit to end.**

Top of bootee

Next row: knit 13 sts.

Next row: knit to last 2 sts, inc in next st, K1.

Next row: knit.

Rep last 2 rows until you have 18 sts on needle.

Work 6 rows in GS. Cast off.

Rejoin yarn to rem 13 sts and work other side of top to match, reversing incs.

Duckling head (make 2)

Using yellow yarn, cast on 10 sts.

Row 1: purl.

Row 2: inc in each st to end.

Row 3: purl.

Row 4: *K1, inc in next st*, rep from * to * to end of row.

Row 5: purl.

Rows 6–13: SS.

Row 14: *K1, K2tog*, rep from * to * to end of row.

Row 15: purl.

Row 16: K2tog across row.

Row 17: purl.

Row 18: K2tog across row. Break yarn and run through sts left on needle, draw up tightly and fasten off.

Beak (make 2)

Using orange yarn, cast on 7 sts.

Knit 1 row and cast off.

Making up

Weave in all loose ends. Using flat seams, join the underfoot, heel and back seams. Turn the top back to form a cuff. Stitch the side seam of each duckling head, stuffing as you do so, forming each head into a neat little ball shape. Take a beak, work in the ends carefully, fold it in half lengthways and sew it to one of the heads. With black yarn, embroider tiny eyes either side of the beak. Make another head to match. Sew a head firmly to the front so that the baby cannot pull them off.

These adorable boot cuffs are sure to warm your heart. The smaller pair will fit a child's boots and the larger pair a woman's wellies or wide, long boots. Sizes and colours can be adjusted to suit your boot.

LOVE MY BOOT CUFFS

Materials:

Child's size: 2 balls of light worsted (DK/8-ply) pure alpaca yarn in red (A); 50g/109yd/100m

1 ball of worsted (aran/10-ply) textured yarn in black (A) and white (B); 50g/104yd/95m

Woman's size: 1 ball of light worsted (DK/8-ply) pure alpaca yarn in red (C); 50g/109yd/100m

1 ball of worsted (aran/10-ply) textured yarn in dark green (D); 50g/104yd/95m

Needles:

1 pair of 5mm (UK 6, US 8) knitting needles

Instructions:

Child's cuff (make 2)

Using 5mm (UK 6; US 8) needles, cast on 48sts in A.

Rows 1–18: *k2, p2*, rep to the end of row.

Work the patterned section.

Woman's cuff (make 2)

Using 5mm (UK 6; US 8) needles, cast on 60sts in C.

Rows 1–22: *k2, p2*, rep to the end of row.

Work the patterned section.

Child's cuff

Continue knitting in colour A.

Rows 1–4: stocking stitch starting with a knit row.

Woman's cuff

Continue knitting in colour A.

Rows 1–6: stocking stitch starting with a knit row.

Woman's and child's cuffs

Using the chart, insert the heart motif. Note that you will be working from the top down so the heart is in the correct position once the boot cuff is on the leg.

Row 1: k3A *k2B, k2A, k2B, k6A*; rep to last 9sts, k2A, k2B, k2A, k3A.

Rows 2–8: Follow the chart for these rows, ending with a purl row.

Rows 9–10: Work st st.

Row 11: k1A, k1B, k10A, *k1B, k11A* rep to end.

Row 12: p10A, *p3B, p9A*, rep to last 14sts, p3B, p8A, p3B.

Row 13: As row 11, cut off yarn B.

Rows 14–16: Work st st in colour A, starting with a purl row.

Row 17: Cast off.

Making up

Sew in loose ends by weaving them into stitches at the back of your work. With right side facing, use a mattress stitch to join side seams of the pattern component of the boot cuff. Sew up rib on the rear side of the boot cuff.

	8	7	6	5	4	3	2	1	
8		■	■			■	■		8
7		■	■	■		■	■	■	7
6		■	■	■	■	■	■	■	6
5		■	■	■	■	■	■	■	5
4			■	■	■	■	■		4
3				■	■	■			3
2					■				2
1					■				1
	8	7	6	5	4	3	2	1	

Get Fruity
Why not enjoy this tempting tea cosy with fruity cakes and tea?

STRAWBERRY TEA COSY

Gauge (tension)
5 sts = 1in (2.5cm).

Instructions:

Make two.

Using red yarn and 4mm (UK 8, US 6) needles, cast on 42 sts.

Knit in SS until work measures 15cm (6in) from the cast on edge.

Shape the top
Row 1: k7, k2tog, *k6, k2tog*, rep from * to * to last st, k1.

Row 2: purl.

Row 3: k6, k2tog, *k5, k2tog*, rep from * to * to last st, k1.

Row 4: purl.

Row 5: k5, k2tog, *k4, k2tog*, rep from * to * to last st, k1.

Row 6: purl.

Row 7: k4, k2tog, *k3, k2tog*, rep from * to * to last st, k1.

Row 8: purl.

Row 9: k3, k2tog, *k2, k2tog*, rep from * to * to last st, k1.

Row 10: purl.

Row 11: k2, k2tog, *k1, k2tog*, rep from * to * to last st, k1.

Row 12: purl.

Row 13: k1, k2tog, *k2tog*, rep from * to * to last st, k1.

Row 14: purl.

Row 15: change to green for stem and k1, k2tog, k1, k2tog, k1.

Row 16: purl.

Row 17: knit.

Row 18: purl.

Row 19: knit.

Cut yarn and place sts on stitch holder.

Materials:
1 ball of worsted (aran/10-ply) yarn in red, and oddments in green and white; 50g/93yd/85m
Two stitch holders

Needles:
1 pair of 4mm (UK 8, US 6) knitting needles and 1 pair of 4mm (UK 8, US 6) DPN

Making up
Place the wrong sides of the cosy together (right sides facing out). Thread a tapestry needle with the green tail on the back stitch holder. Graft the sts on the stitch holders together.

Sew the stem
Continuing with the green tail of yarn, sew down one side of the stem. Fasten off and hide tail in seam. Repeat on other side of stem.

Sew the top
Thread a tapestry needle with one of the red tails at the top of the cosy. Sew down one side for 3in (7.5cm). Fasten off and hide tail in the seam. Repeat on other side of the cosy.

Sew the bottom
Thread a tapestry needle with one of the red tails of yarn from the cast on edge. Sew up one side for 1½in (4cm). Fasten off and hide tail in the seam. Repeat on the other side of the cosy.

Leaves (make 5)
Using green yarn and the 4mm (UK 8, US 6) DPN, cast on 2 sts.

Rows 1–8: knit.

Row 9: k1, m1, k1.

Rows 10–15: knit.

Row 16: k1, m1, k1, m1, k1.

Row 17–22: knit.

Row 23: k1, m1, k3, m1, k1.

Rows 24–27: knit.

Row 28: k1, k2tog, k1, k2tog, k1.

Row 29: k2tog, k1, k2tog.

Row 30: sk2po.

Fasten off.

Attach the leaves
Position the leaves on the base of the stem and sew in place. Work in ends neatly.

Make the seeds
Using white yarn, embroider small, V-shaped patterns randomly around the cosy.

MINI SNOWMAN

Materials:

1 ball of fingering (4-ply) yarn in sparkly white, and small amounts in brown, green, black and orange; 50g/191yd/175m

Small amount of self-patterning fingering (4-ply) yarn for scarf

Toy stuffing

Needles:

1 pair of 2.75mm (UK 12, US 2) DPN

Size:

Approx. 3⅛in (8cm) tall

White Christmas

This snowman has a cool blue look with his colour-coordinated hat and scarf set. You can use up your odds and ends of yarn dressing up these snowmen, as long as you have enough white!

Instructions:

Body

Using sparkly white yarn, cast on 14 sts, P 1 row.

Work increase rows as follows:

K1, (K1fb, K1, K1fb) to last st, K1. P 1 row (22 sts).

K1, (K1fb, K3, K1fb) to last st, K1. P 1 row (30 sts).

K1, (K1fb, K5, K1fb) to last st, K1. P 1 row (38 sts).

K1, (K1fb, K7, K1fb) to last st, K1. P 1 row (46 sts).

K1, (K1fb, K9, K1fb) to last st, K1. P 1 row (54 sts).

Work 2 rows in SS. Work decrease rows as follows:

K1, (K2tog, K9, ssk) to last st, K1. P1 row (46 sts).

K1, (K2tog, K7, ssk) to last st, K1. P1 row (38 sts).

K1, (K2tog, K5, ssk) to last st, K1. P1 row (30 sts).

K1, (K2tog, K3, ssk) to last st, K1. P1 row (22 sts).

K1, (K2tog, K1, ssk) to last st, K1. P1 row (14 sts).

Thread yarn through rem sts and fasten off.

Head

Using sparkly white yarn, cast on 14 sts, P 1 row.

Work inc rows as follows:

K1, (K1fb, K1, K1fb) to last st, K1. P 1 row (22 sts).

K1, (K1fb, K3, K1fb) to last st, K1. P 1 row (30 sts).

K1, (K1fb, K5, K1fb) to last st, K1. P 1 row (38 sts).

K1, (K1fb, K7, K1fb) to last st, K1. P 1 row (46 sts).

Work decrease rows as follows:

K1, (K2tog, K7, ssk) to last st, K1. P 1 row (38 sts).

K1, (K2tog, K5, ssk) to last st, K1. P 1 row (30 sts).K1, (K2tog, K3, ssk) to last st, K1. P 1 row (22 sts).

K1, (K2tog, K1, ssk) to last st, K1. P 1 row (14 sts).

Thread yarn through rem sts and fasten off.

Nose

Using orange yarn, cast on 5 sts.

P 1 row.

K2tog, K1, K2tog (3 sts).

Sl1, K2tog, psso.

Fasten off rem st.

Hat

Using green yarn, cast on 5 sts.

Next row: K1, (M1, K1) to last st, M1, K1 (9 sts).

P 1 row.

Rep the last 2 rows twice more (33 sts).

P 1 row (RS).

Starting with a P row, work 7 rows in SS.

Next row: (K2, M1) to last st, K1 (49 sts).

P 1 row.

Work 3 rows in GS. Cast off.

Arms (make 2)

Using brown yarn, cast on 4 sts and work an i-cord 1in (2.5cm) long (see page 18). Work a second i-cord just ¼in (0.5cm) long and sew it on to the first i-cord to make a 'forked' hand.

Scarf

Using self-patterning yarn, cast on 7 sts and work 4in (10cm) in GS. Cast off.

Making up

Stuff and sew the side seams of the body and head. Attach the head to the body. Sew on the arms. Sew the side seam of the hat and sew it on to the snowman's head. Sew up the nose and attach. Using French knots, embroider the eyes and buttons with black yarn and a darning needle. Tie the scarf around the snowman's neck.

CHERRY BLOSSOM

Materials:

Oddments of light worsted (DK/8-ply) bamboo
   yarn in very pale pink

Pearl stamens

Needles:

1 pair of 3mm (UK 11, US 2) knitting needles

Size:

Approx. 2in (5cm) across

Instructions:

Petal (make 5)

Cast on 5 sts.

Row 1: k4, turn, leaving rem st on needle.

Row 2: p3, turn, leaving rem st on needle.

Row 3: k3, turn.

Row 4: p3, turn.

Row 5: k4.

Row 6: p2tog, p1, p2tog (3 sts).

Row 7: k1, k2tog, psso.

Fasten off.

Making up

Join the petals at the centre, inserting stamens and
securing them with a few stitches.

Opposite

*The perfect choice for a bridesmaid, stitch one or
more blossoms to a hair slide or clip for a pretty hair
decoration, or to a length of ribbon to make a choker or
wrist corsage. For an alternative, use light worsted (DK/8-
ply) cotton yarn in a bright pink and, instead of stamens,
stitch a few seed beads in the centre of the flower.*

POPPY PANDA BEAR

Materials:

- 1 ball each of light worsted (DK/8-ply) yarn in black and white; 50g/137yd/125m
- Toy stuffing
- 2 x 6mm round black beads for eyes
- Black embroidery thread or floss for features
- 9¾in (25cm) narrow red satin ribbon

Tools:

- 1 pair of 3.25mm (UK 10, US 3) knitting needles
- Sewing needle
- Stitch holder

Instructions:

Make the bear following the instructions on page 41, but do not attach the eyes. Knit the head using white yarn, and the arms using black. When working the body, begin with black yarn, continue until all shaping is complete, then change to white yarn. Continue with white until you divide for the legs, then change to black yarn. Complete the legs using black. Make both sides to match.

Eye patches (make 2)

Using black yarn, cast on 3 sts.

Row 1: knit.

Row 2: inc 1 st at each end of row.

Rows 3–6: GS.

Row 7: dec 1 st at each end of row.

Row 8: knit.

Row 9: sl1, k2tog, psso.

Fasten off.

Ears (make 2)

Using black yarn, cast on 3 sts.

Row 1: knit.

Row 2: inc 1 st at each end of row.

Rows 3–8: GS.

Row 9: dec 1 st at each end of row.

Row 10: knit.

Row 11: sl1, k2tog, psso.

Fasten off.

Making up

Position the eye patches either side of the bear's nose, using the photograph as a guide, and stitch them in place. Sew the eyes on top of the patches. Fold the ears in half, and place them over the ears that form part of the bear's head. Gather them slightly into shape and secure. Tie a piece of red ribbon around the bear's neck.

This cheeky sheep looks great poking out of the top of a pocket or a bag.

CURIOUS SHEEP PHONE SOCK

Materials:

1 ball of light worsted (DK/8-ply) bouclé yarn in cream; 50g/109yd/100m

Oddment of light worsted (DK/8-ply) yarn in black

2 x seed beads for eyes

White embroidery thread for mouth

Small amount of toy stuffing

Snap fastening

Tools:

1 pair of 4mm (UK 8, US 6) and 1 pair of 3.5mm (UK 9, US 4) knitting needles

Scissors

Tape measure

Embroidery needle

Instructions:

Sock

Using 4mm (UK 8, US 6) needles, cast on 16 sts in cream and work garter stitch for 3½in (9cm).

Next row: Cast on 8 sts at the beginning of the row, then continue in garter stitch until the work measures 6in (15cm) from the beginning of the work. Cast off. Close the side and lower seams.

Sheep head (make 1)

Using 3.5mm (UK 9, US 4) needles, cast on 9 sts in black.

Rows 1–10: st st, starting with a knit row, leaving a long tail.

Draw the tail through the stitches, and take the work off the needle. Stuff the head, then close the back of it. Attach seed beads for the eyes, then embroider a nose and mouth as shown using white thread.

Sheep ears (make 2)

Using 3.5mm (UK 9, US 4) needles, cast on 3 sts in black.

Rows 1–4: knit.

Draw up as for the head.

Sheep legs (make 2)

Using 3.5mm (UK 9, US 4) needles, cast on 3 sts in black.

Rows 1–8: knit.

Cast off.

Making up

Use the embroidery needle and thread to attach the ears to the head, then attach the head to the body in the centre of the flap. Roll each leg into a cylinder shape and attach them to the corners of the sock flap as shown opposite, using the embroidery needle and thread. Close the side seams using mattress stitch, then attach a snap fastening to finish (see detail above) using the embroidery needle and thread.

WARM AND WOOLLY MUG HUG

Materials:

1 ball of fingering (4-ply) yarn in blue, and an oddment in black; 50g/191yd/175m

Oddment of bouclé yarn in white

1 blue flower button

Needles:

1 pair 3.25mm (UK 10, US 3) and 1 pair 3.75mm (UK 9, US 5) knitting needles

Size:

Approx. 7¾ x 3¼in (20 x 8cm)

Note: This pattern produces very stretchy knitting, so the mug hug can fit a
  slightly larger mug than the given measurements.

*As a complete contrast to the
main pattern, try the alternative
(opposite) using black yarn and a
pretty rose design, following the
instructions on page 187.*

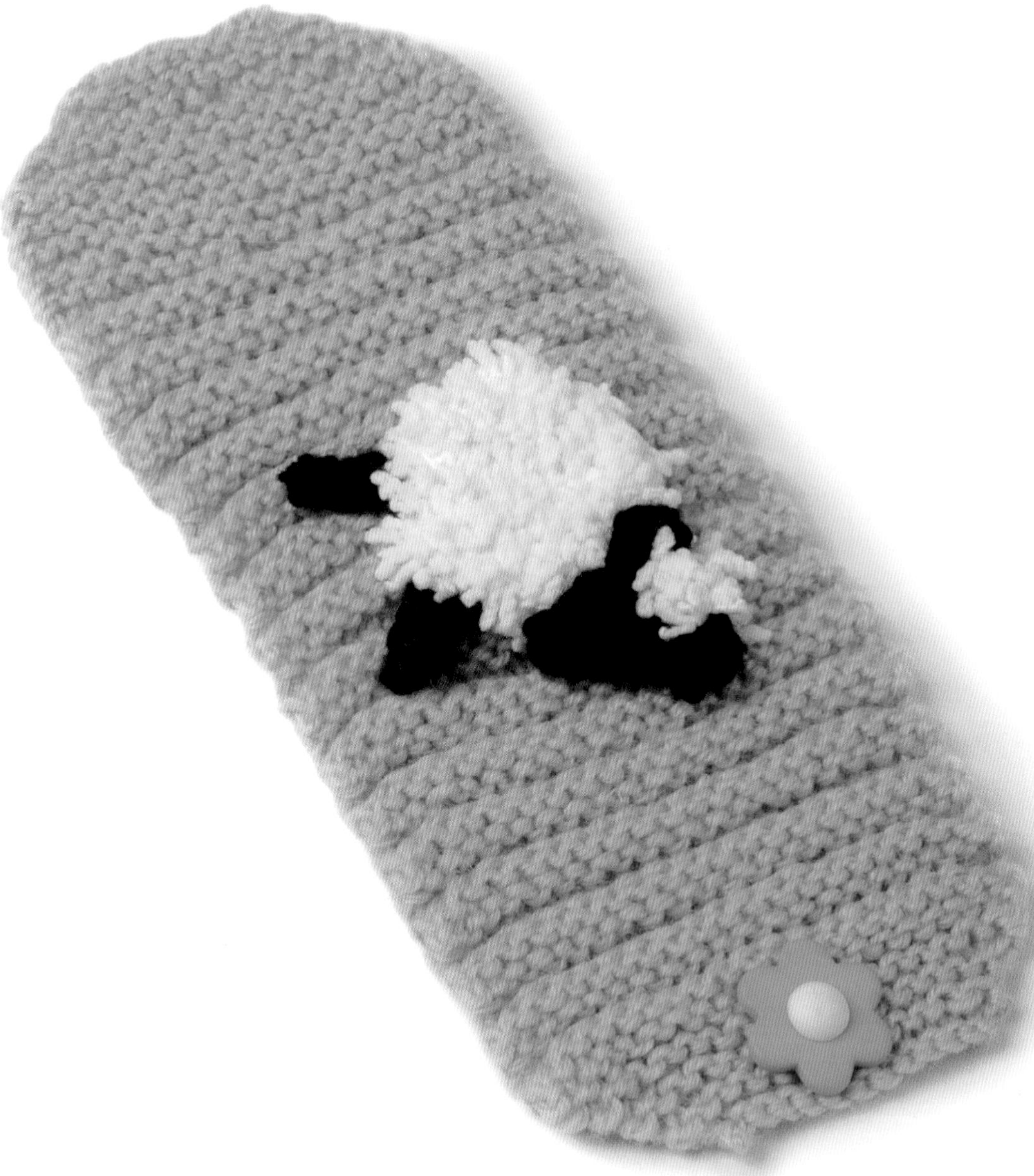

Instructions:

Using blue yarn and 3.25mm (UK 10, US 3) needles, cast on 11 sts.

Knit 1 row.

Working in GS, inc 1 st at each end of next and every alt row until 21 sts on needle.

Commence pattern as follows:

Row 1: knit.

Rows 2–3: purl.

Row 4: knit.

Rep rows 1–4 until work measures 6¾in (17cm), ending on row 4.

Change to GS and shape end.

Dec 1 st at each end of next and every alt row until 15 sts rem.

Next row: to make buttonhole, K2tog, K5, yrn, K2tog, knit to last 2 sts, K2tog.

Next row: knit, knitting into the yrn of the previous row.

Continue in GS. Dec as before until 11 sts rem. Cast off.

Sheep's body

Using bouclé yarn and 3.75mm (UK 9, US 5) needles, cast on 8 sts.

Purl 1 row.

Next row: knit, inc 1 st at each end of row.

Work 5 rows in SS.

Dec 1 st at each end of next and every alt row until 2 sts rem. Cast off.

Legs (make 2)

Using 3.25mm (UK 10, US 3) needles and black yarn, cast on 8 sts.

Knit 1 row. Cast off.

Head

Using 3.25mm (UK 10, US 3) needles and black yarn, cast on 12 sts.

Working in GS, knit 2 rows.

Rows 3–4: cast off 3 sts at beg of row (6 sts).

Rows 5–8: knit.

Row 9: K2tog, K2, K2tog (4 sts).

Row 10: K2tog twice.

Row 11: K2tog. Fasten off.

Making up

Work in all ends neatly. Place the sheep's body on to the centre of the mug hug and stitch it in place. Tuck the tops of the legs under the body and secure. Attach the head to the body. Wind a short length of bouclé yarn into a small coil and sew it to the top of the sheep's head. Sew on the button to correspond with the buttonhole at the other end.

Alternative design

To make the rose on the glamorous alternative design:

Using size 3.25mm (UK 10, US 3) needles and pink yarn, cast on 12 sts.

Row 1: purl.

Row 2: K10, turn and purl to end.

Row 3: K8, turn and purl to end.

Row 4: K6, turn and purl to end.

Row 5: K4, turn and purl to end.

Row 6: K2, turn and purl to end.

Row 7: knit.

Row 8: purl.

Rep rows 2–8 ten more times.

Cast off.

Make two leaves, worked in GS, as follows:

Using the same needles and green yarn, cast on 5 sts. Knit 1 row.

Inc 1 st at each end of next and every alt row until 11 sts on needle.

Knit 4 rows.

Dec 1 st at each end of every row until 3 sts rem.

K3tog, fasten off.

Making up

Coil the rose into a tight spiral and fold over the outer edges to form petals. Sew together at the join. Stitch a few glass beads on to the rose to form dew drops. Sew the leaves together and stitch them to the back of the rose. Sew the completed flower to the centre of a black mug hug. Sew on a black button to correspond with the buttonhole.

CUPCAKE EGG COSY

Instructions:

Top of cupcake

Cast on 36 sts in chocolate yarn using 2.75mm (UK 12, US 2) needles.

Rows 1–6: st st.

Rows 7–18: change to pink and work in g st.

Row 19: knit, decreasing 4 sts randomly across row (32 sts).

Row 20: knit.

Row 21: knit, decreasing 4 sts randomly across row (28 sts).

Row 22: knit.

Row 23: knit, decreasing 4 sts randomly across row (24 sts).

Row 24: knit.

Row 25: knit, decreasing 4 sts randomly across row (20 sts).

Row 26: knit.

Break yarn, leaving a long end. Thread through stitches on needle and draw up tightly.

Side of case

Cast on 60 sts using white cotton yarn and 2.25mm (UK 13, US 1) needles.

Rows 1–11: (K1, P1) to end of row.

Row 12: inc every second P st across row.

Cast off.

Making up

Join the two sides of the case and the cupcake top. Pull up the thread holding the stitches at the top of the cake, and darn the thread end in to hold it firmly in place. Stitch the case to the cake top. Using lime green wool, work sets of four lazy daisy stitches randomly over the top of the cake. If you enjoy a larger breakfast egg, knit the cosy using larger needles!

Why not make a complete set of these stylish egg cosies to match your own kitchen. This alternative design has been made using blue and cream yarn and has dark blue embroidered lazy daisy stitches.

Materials:

1 ball each of fingering (4-ply) pure merino yarn in chocolate and pink, plus oddments in lime green; 50g/191yd/175m

1 ball of fingering (4-ply) pure cotton yarn in white; 50g/147yd/135m

Needles:

1 pair of 2.75mm (UK 12, US 2) and 1 pair of 2.25mm (UK 13, US 1) knitting needles

VERNA ALIEN

Materials:

1 ball each of light worsted (DK/8-ply) yarn in light brown and variegated green; 50g/137yd/125m

Oddment of purple yarn

Three pairs of beads for eyes

Toy stuffing

Sewing thread

Needles:

1 pair of 3mm (UK 11, US 2) knitting needles

Sewing needle

Instructions:

Face (make 3)

Cast on 3 sts in light brown.

Row 1: inc each st (6 sts).

Row 2: purl.

Row 3: inc each st (12 sts).

Rows 4–6: st st.

Row 7: k5, inc in each of next 2 sts, k5 (14 sts).

Rows 8–10: st st.

Row 11: k5, k2tog twice, k5 (12 sts).

Rows 12–14: st st.

Row 15: k2tog along row (6 sts).

Row 16: purl.

Row 17: k2tog along row (3 sts).

Row 18: purl and cast off.

Leaves (make 4)

Cast on 2 sts in variegated green.

Row 1: inc each st (4 sts).

Row 2: purl.

Row 3: inc each st (8 sts).

Row 4: purl.

Row 5: inc each st (16 sts).

Row 6: purl.

Row 7: cast off 3 sts at beg of row, k to end (13 sts).

Row 8: cast off 3 sts at beg of row, p to end (10 sts).

Row 9: cast on 3 sts at beg of row, k to end (13 sts).

Row 10: cast on 3 sts at beg of row, p to end (16 sts).

Row 11: cast off 5 sts at beg of row, k to end (11 sts).

Row 12: cast off 5 sts at beg of row, p to end (6 sts).

Rows 13–15: st st.

Row 16: p2tog (5 sts).

Row 17: knit and cast off.

Making up

Place two faces together and sew up side seam to the top. Place the third face between the two faces and stitch up each side seam to the top of the head. Stuff and sew the base shut. Needlesculpt each nose and sew on eyes, then embroider mouths. Stitch two leaves on top and two on the bottom.

Verna aliens are very inquisitive. To keep them safe from harm, they have three faces on their bodies, so they can see all around themselves at once.

ASPARAGUS

Materials:

1 ball of fingering (4-ply) wool, acrylic or blended yarn in moss green, and small amounts in in pale green and pale peach; 50g/191yd/175m

Toy stuffing

Needles:

Set of four 2.75mm (UK12, US 2) DPN

Size:

Approx. 7½ x ⅞in (19 x 2.25cm)

Instructions:

Using moss green yarn, cast on 6 sts and distribute these equally between three needles.

Round 1: k.

Round 2: inc1 in each st (12 sts).

Round 3: (k3, inc1) three times (15 sts).

Rounds 4–73: k.

Round 74: (k3, k2tog) three times (12 sts).

Rounds 75–79: k.

Round 80: (k2, k2tog) three times (9 sts).

Rounds 81–83: k.

Round 84: (k1, k2tog) three times (6 sts).

Rounds 85–87: k.

Round 88: k2tog three times (3 sts).

Round 89: k3tog, break yarn and fasten off.

Making up

Fill the stalk with toy stuffing and stitch the ends closed. Count down 13 rounds from the tip and pick up 4 sts on one double-pointed needle. Slide the loops to one end and, with a second needle and pale green yarn, proceed as follows:

Row 1: k1, (inc1) twice, k1 (6 sts).

Row 2: p to end; break yarn and continue in moss green yarn.

Beg with a k row, work 4 rows in st st; break yarn and continue in pale peach yarn.

Row 7: k1, (k2tog) twice, k1 (4 sts).

Row 8: p.

Row 9: k1, k2tog, k1 (3 sts).

Row 10: p3tog; fasten off.

Repeat twice more on the same round, then add a few more at intervals further down the stalk.

Asparagus Stalks

There are different varieties of asparagus. Knit one using white or ivory yarn for the main stalk, with pale peach and lilac for the bracts.

BLACKBERRY

Instructions:

Before starting to knit, thread 90 beads on to yarn.

With 2mm (UK 14, US 0) needles and prepared yarn, cast on 10 sts.

Row 1: k each st tbl.

Row 2: k1, inc1 in each st to end (19 sts).

Row 3: *k1, insert needle into next st, push 1 bead to back of st just worked, complete k st, rep from * to last st, k1.

Row 4: p1, insert needle purlwise into next st, push one bead up to front of st just worked, then complete p st; rep from * to end.

Rows 5–12: rep rows 3 and 4.

Row 13: k1, (k2tog) nine times (10 sts).

Cut yarn and thread through rem sts.

Stalk

With 2mm (UK 14, US 0) double-pointed needles and green fingering (4-ply) yarn, cast on 2 sts.

Row 1: k2; do not turn but slide sts to other end of needle.

Rep row 1 nine times more; cast off.

Making up

Complete the blackberry by stitching the edges (row ends) together to form a tube, then pull up the yarn to gather the top, trapping one end of the stalk. Knot a few short strands of green yarn around the base of the stalk and trim each strand to about $\frac{1}{8}$in (3mm). The finished blackberry measures approximately $\frac{7}{8}$in (2.25cm) high, excluding the stalk.

Blackberry Surprise

Try varying the colours of the beads and the yarn as you make a punnet's worth. Unripe blackberries are red, so try using all red beads, or half red and half purple. These small variations will make the group look more natural.

Materials:

1 ball of fingering (4-ply) wool or wool blend yarn in navy blue; 50g/191yd/175m

Small amount of light worsted (DK/8-ply) wool or wool blend yarn in green

Toy stuffing

Size 9/0 glass rocaille beads in purple

Needles:

1 pair of 2mm (UK 14, US 0) knitting needles and 1 pair of 2mm (UK 14, US 0) DPN

TWO-TONE CABLE HEADBAND

Materials:

1 ball of light worsted (DK/8-ply) Bluefaced
   Leicester in black/brown tweed look (A);
   50g/112yd/102m

1 ball of light worsted (DK/8-ply) superfine
   alpaca yarn in black (B); 50g/131yd/120m

Needles:

1 pair of 4mm (UK 8, US 6) knitting needles

1 x cable needle

Instructions:

Using yarn A, cast on 29 sts, then ktbl to form a
neat edge.

Note: the first 10 and last 10 sts are worked in yarn A
and the middle 9 sts in yarn B.

Cable pattern

Remember to twist yarns every time you change
colours to avoid gaps in your knitting.

Rows 1 and 5: k10A, k9B, k10A.

Rows 2, 4, 6 and 8: k1A, p9A, p9B, p9A, k1A.

Row 3: k1A, *slip next 3 sts onto a cable needle and
hold at back of work, k3A, k3A from cable needle**,
k3A, rep from * to ** in yarn B, k3B, rep from * to ** in
yarn A, k4A.

Row 7: k4A, *slip 3 sts onto a cable needle and hold
at front of work, k3A, k3A from cable needle**, k3B,
rep from * to ** in yarn B, k3A, rep from * to ** in
yarn A, k1A.

Continue the 8-row cable pattern until the headband fits
snugly around your head with a slight stretch, ending on
row 8 of pattern.

Knit 1 row in yarn A.

Cast off all sts.

Making up
With RS facing, join seams together using mattress
stitch. Weave in all loose ends.

*I have used a two-tone cable for this pattern
to give it a certain panache. If preferred,
it could be done in a single colour. This
headband is particularly versatile and would
suit all family members.*

SPARKLER CUFFS

Materials:

1 ball of light worsted (DK/8-ply) beaded yarn in turquoise; 100g/273yd/250m

Needles:

1 pair of 4mm (UK 8, US 6) and 1 pair of 3.5mm (UK 9 or 10, US 4) knitting needles

Instructions:

Make two. Using 4mm (UK 8, US 6) needles, cast on 37 sts, then ktbl to form a neat edge.

Next row: k3 *MB, k5*, rep from * to * to last 4 sts, MB, k3.

MB: Make a bobble all in the same stitch. Knit into front, back and front again of same st, turn. Sl1, k1, psso, k1, pass previous st over. You are now back to the original 1 stitch.

Main pattern

Row 1 and every odd-numbered row (WS): Purl.

Row 2: *k10, sl1, k1, psso, yfwd*, rep from * to * to last st, k1.

Row 4: k9, sl1, k1, psso, yfwd, *k10, sl1, k1, psso, yfwd*, rep from * to * to last 2 sts, k2.

Row 6: *k8, (sl1, k1, psso, yfwd) twice*, rep from * to * to last st, k1.

Row 8: k7, (sl1, k1, psso, yfwd) twice, *k8, (sl1, k1, psso, yfwd) twice*, rep from * to * to last 2 sts, k2.

Row 10: *k6, (sl1, k1, psso, yfwd) three times*, rep from * to * to last st, k1.

Row 12: k5, (sl1, k1, psso, yfwd) three times, *k6, (sl1, k1, psso, yfwd) three times*, rep from * to * to last 2 sts, k2.

Row 14: *k4, (sl1, k1, psso, yfwd) four times*, rep from * to * to last st, k1.

Row 16: k1, *yfwd, k2tog, k10*, rep from * to * to end of row.

Row 18: k2, yfwd, k2tog, *k10, yfwd, k2tog*, rep from * to * to last 9 sts, k9.

Row 20: k1, *(yfwd, k2tog) twice, k8*, rep from * to * to end of row.

Row 22: k2, (yfwd, k2tog) twice, *k8, (yfwd, k2tog) twice*, rep from * to * to last 7 sts, k7.

Row 24: k1, *(yfwd, k2tog) three times, k6*, rep from * to * to end of row.

Row 26: k2, (yfwd, k2tog) three times, *k6 (yfwd, k2tog) three times*, rep from * to * to last 5 sts, k5.

Row 28: k1, *(yfwd, k2tog) four times, k4*, rep from * to * to end of row.

Repeat rows 1–17 once more.

Change to 3.5mm (UK 9 or 10/US 4) needles.

Next row: *k1, p1*, rep from * to * to last st, k1.

Next row: p1, *k1, p1*, rep from * to * to end of row.

Cast off all stitches.

Making up

Join the side seams using a tapestry needle and mattress stitch, 2¾in (7cm) from the wrist end (cast-on edge) and 2in (5cm) from the finger end. This will leave a gap for your thumb to go through. Weave in all loose ends.

These are really pretty beaded cuffs that will brighten up any outfit. The bobbles around the cuff add a little more texture to the fabric.

This is a funky little scarf that cleverly ruches in panels. I have made it in traditional black and white using ultra-soft alpaca wool.

ZEBRA RAZZLE SCARF

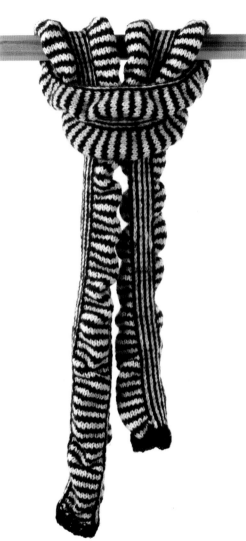

Materials:

4 x 50g balls of light worsted (DK/8-ply) yarn: 3 x
black (A), 1 x parchment (B); 50g/144yd/132m

Needles:

1 pair of 4.5mm (UK 7, US 7) and 1 pair of 4mm
(UK 8, US 6) knitting needles

Instructions:

Initial rows

Rows 1–2: Using 4mm (UK 8, US 6) needles and yarn A,
cast on 49 sts, ktbl on return row (i.e. row 2).

Rib section:

Row 1: *k1, p1*, repeat to last st, k1.

Row 2: *p1, k1*, repeat to last st, p1.

Rows 3–4: Repeat rows 1 and 2.

Stripe pattern section

Change to 4.5mm (UK 7; US 7) needles.

Row 1: To set the pattern, purl 1 row in colour A.

Row 2: (Right side) Using colour B, (k1, sl1) five times;
k10, sl1, (k1, sl1) four times, repeat * to * once more
to last st, k1.

Row 3: Using colour B, (p1, sl1) five times, *p10, sl1
(p1, sl1) four times*, repeat from * to * once more to
last st, p1.

Row 4: Using colour A, k2, sl1, (k1, sl1) three times;
k12, sl1, (k1, sl1) three times, repeat * to * once more
to last 2 sts, k2.

Row 5: Using colour A, p2, sl1, (p1, sl1) three times;
p12, sl1, (p1, sl1) three times, repeat * to * once more
to last 2 sts, p2.

Next rows: Continue in set pattern (rows 2–5 only) until
work measures approximately 62¼in (158cm), ending
with a row 5. Cut off yarn B.

Next row: Change to size 4mm (UK 8, US 6) needles
and knit in yarn A.

Next 4 rows: Work rows 1–4 of the rib section as you
did at the start of the scarf.

Cast off your stitches.

Making up

Sew in loose ends by weaving them into the back of
your scarf.

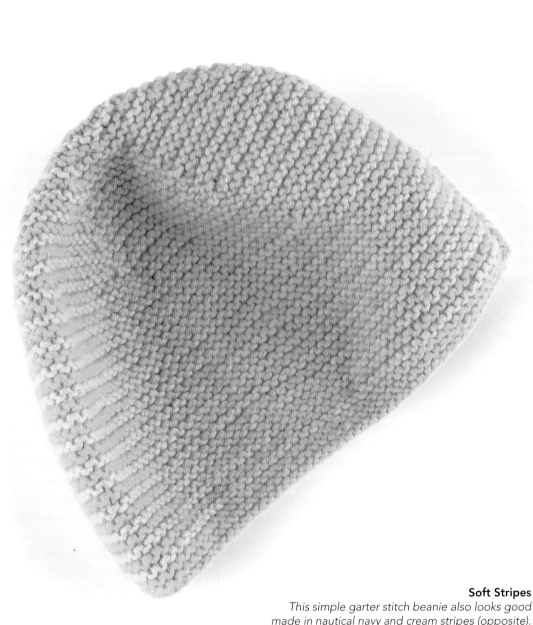

Soft Stripes

This simple garter stitch beanie also looks good made in nautical navy and cream stripes (opposite). Work the last 16–18 rows in plain cream, then make four navy pompoms (see page 19). Trim them to size with scissors and stitch them to the centre of the crown. This pattern is for an adult hat, but by working it in a fingering (4-ply) yarn using 2.75mm (UK 12, US 2) and 3.25mm (UK 10, US 3) needles, you can produce a child-size version.

KNIT KNIT BEANIE

Materials:

1 ball each of light worsted (DK/8-ply)) cotton blend yarn in lime green (A) and turquoise (B); 50g/124yd/113m

Needles:

1 pair of 3mm (UK 11, US 3) and 1 pair of 3.75mm (UK 9, US 5) knitting needles

Size:

To fit an average adult female head

Gauge (tension)

23 sts and 24 rows to 4in (10cm), using 3.75mm (UK 9, US 5) knitting needles, measured over garter stitch.

Instructions:

Using 3mm needles and yarn B, cast on 112 sts.

Row 1: (k1, p1) to end.

Rep row 1 three times more.

Change to 3.75mm needles.

Rows 5 and 6: knit, using A; do not cut A but pick up B.

Rows 7 and 8: knit, using B; do not cut B but pick up A.

Rep rows 5–8 eight times more.

Row 41: (k13, k3tog) seven times (98 sts).

Still changing colours after every alt row, work a further 9 rows.

Row 51: (k11, k3tog) seven times (84 sts).

Still changing colours after every alt row, work a further 7 rows.

Row 59: (k9, k3tog) seven times (70 sts).

Still changing colours after every alt row, work a further 5 rows.

Row 65: (k7, k3tog) seven times (56 sts).

Still changing colours after every alt row, work a further 5 rows.

Row 71: (k5, k3tog) seven times (42 sts).

Still changing colours after every alt row, work a further 3 rows.

Row 75: (k1, k2tog) fourteen times (28 sts).

Knit 1 row.

Row 77: (k2tog) fourteen times.

Knit 1 row.

Row 79: (k2tog) seven times.

Cut yarn and thread tail through rem 7 sts.

Making up

With right sides together and using the tails of yarn, stitch up the back seam in backstitch; turn right sides out.

ROSIE TOES BOOTEES

Materials:

1 ball of light worsted (DK/8-ply) baby yarn
in white, and an oddment in pale pink;
50g/115yd/105m

2 x pink ribbon rose motifs

40in (1m) of narrow pink baby ribbon

Needles:

1 pair of 3.75mm (UK 9, US 5) knitting needles

Instructions:

Make two.

Using white yarn, cast on 27 sts.

Row 1: knit.

Row 2: K2, m1, K11, m1, K1, m1, K11, m1, K2 (31 sts).

Row 3: knit.

Row 4: K2, m1, K12, m1, K3, m1, K12, m1, K2.

Row 5: knit.

Row 6: K2, m1, K13, m1, K5, m1, K13, m1, K2.

Row 7: knit.

Row 8: K2, m1, K14, m1, K7, m1, K14, m1, K2.

Row 9: knit.

Join in pink yarn and work picot border as follows:

Rows 10–13: SS.

Row 14: K1, *yfwd, K2tog*, rep from * to * to end
of row.

Row 15: purl.

Rows 16–17: knit.

Break pink and rejoin white.

Rows 18–29: GS.

Shape instep as follows:

Row 30: K26, turn.

Row 31: K9, turn.

Row 32: K8, K2tog, turn.

Row 33: K8, K2togtbl, turn.

Rows 34–43: rep rows 32 and 33 five times, turn.

Row 44: K9, knit across rem sts on left-hand needle.

Row 45: knit.

Work 18 rows in GS.

Break white and join in pink.

Work picot edging as follows:

Work 3 rows in SS.

Next row: K1, *yfwd, K2tog*, rep from * to * to end
of row.

Next row: purl.

Work 4 rows in SS. Cast off loosely.

Making up

Work in all the yarn ends. Working with the wrong sides
facing, sew up the pink picot edging by matching the
sides together stitch by stitch. This will form a neat
picot edge on the right side of the work. Sew the seam
on the base of each foot and then join the leg seams,
matching the rows. Fold over the pink picot edging at
the top of each bootee on to the wrong side of the work
and catch it down all around the inside. Cut the ribbon
into two equal lengths and thread a length through the
holes at each ankle. Sew a ribbon rose motif firmly on
to the toe of each bootee, so that the baby cannot pull
them off.

BLUEBERRY BOUCLÉ BOOT CUFFS

Materials:

1 ball each of worsted (aran/10-ply) textured yarn in cream (A), teal (B) and raspberry (C); 100g/204yd/190m

Needles:

1 pair of 5mm (UK 6, US 8) and 1 pair of 6mm (UK 4, US 10) knitting needles

Instructions:

Make two.

Using 5mm (UK 6, US 8) needles, cast on 53 sts in yarn A.

Rib

Row 1: *k2, p2* rep to last st, k1.

Row 2: p1, *k2, p2* rep to end

Rows 3–12: Rep rows 1 and 2.

Main body

Change to 6mm (UK 4, US 10) needles.

Row 1: k1 in yarn A. *Work 1 bobble in yarn B as follows: with B, k1, y/o, pass k st over y/o and return remaining y/o st to left needle, rep twice more, leaving last y/o st on right needle, k1 in yarn A*. Repeat from * to * until end of row. Cut off yarn B.

Row 2: Using yarn A, purl.

Row 3: Using yarn C, work 1 bobble as above *k1 in yarn A, work 1 bobble using colour C*. Rep from * to * until end of row. Cut off yarn C.

Row 4: Using yarn A purl.

Rows 5–8: Rejoin yarn B, knit every row (garter st).

Row 9: As row 3.

Row 10: As row 4.

Row 11: As row 1.

Row 12: As row 2.

Rows 13–16: Rejoin yarn C, knit every row. Cast off sts.

Making up

Sew in loose ends by weaving them into stitches at the back of your work.

With right side facing, use a mattress stitch to join the side seams of the pattern component of the boot cuff. Sew up the rib on the rear side of the boot cuff.

The elongated bobbles give the yarn a bouclé effect and add character to the cuffs.

Love Is In The Air
*What could be better than a
steaming mug of tea to warm your
heart and hands on Valentine's day?*

Materials:

1 ball each of worsted (aran/10-
ply) yarn in white and red;
50g/103yd/94m

Polyester wadding

Tools:

1 pair of 4mm (UK 8, US 6) knitting
needles; 1 pair each of 4mm (UK 8,
US 6) and 3.25mm (UK 10, US 3) DPN

2 stitch holders

Gauge (tension)

5 sts = 2.5cm (1in).

VALENTINE'S DAY TEA COSY

Instructions:

Make two.

Using red yarn and 4mm (UK 8, US 6) needles, cast on 42 sts.

Work 14 rows in SS.

Change to white yarn and continue in SS until cosy measures 6in (15cm) from the cast-on edge.

Shape the top
Row 1: k7, k2tog, *k6, k2tog*, rep from * to * to last st, k1.

Row 2: purl.

Row 3: k6, k2tog, *k5, k2tog*, rep from * to * to last st, k1.

Row 4: purl.

Row 5: knit.

Row 6: purl.

Row 7: k4, yo, k2tog, k4, yo, k2tog, k4, yo, k2tog.

Row 8: purl.

Row 9: knit.

Row 10: purl.

Change to red and continue with SS for 14 rows.

Cast off.

Making up
Place the wrong sides of the cosy together (right sides facing out).

Sew the top
Thread a tapestry needle with one of the white tails.

Sew 2½in (6cm) down one side, starting at the first white row.

Fasten off, hide tail in seam.

Repeat on other side of cosy.

Sew the bottom
Thread a tapestry needle with one of the red tails of yarn from the cast on edge.

Sew up one side for 1½in (4cm).

Fasten off, hide tail in seam.

Repeat on other side of cosy.

Make the hearts
For two hearts make four heart shapes. Using red yarn and 3.25mm (UK 10, US 3) needles, cast on 3 sts.

Row 1: purl.

Row 2: k1, yo, k1, yo, k1.

Row 3: purl.

Row 4: k1, yo, k3, yo, k1.

Row 5: purl.

Row 6: k1, yo, k5, yo, k1.

Row 7: purl.

Row 8: k1, yo, k7, yo, k1.

Row 9: purl.

Row 10: k1, yo, k9, yo, k1.

Row 11: p5, p2tog, p6.

Work the top of the hearts following the directions below.

Do not cut yarn.

First lobe
Row 1: k1, ssk, k1, k2tog.

Slip remaining 6 sts onto st holder.

Row 2: p1, p2tog, p1.

Row 3: knit.

Row 4: sl1 purlwise, p2tog, psso.

Cut yarn and pull through st.

Second lobe
Slip 6 sts from st holder onto needle.

Join yarn.

Row 1: k1, ssk, k1, k2tog.

Row 2: p1, p2tog, p1.

Row 3: knit.

Row 4: sl 1 purlwise, p2tog, psso.

Cut yarn and pull through st.

With tails and a tapestry needle, sew two hearts together (right sides facing out) leaving a small opening at the top of the heart.

Lightly stuff hearts with wadding. Finish sewing.

Hanging cord
Using red yarn and the 4mm (UK 8, US 6) DPN, cast on 3 sts.

Row 1: k3; do not turn but slide sts to other end of needle.

Repeat this row until work measures approximately 10in (25cm). Fasten off.

Weave cord through eyelets at the top of the cosy. Make sure both ends come out of the same eyelet opening. Sew cord ends to hearts, pull cord tight and tie cord into a knot.

WHAT A HOOT

Materials:

Small amount of bulky (chunky) yarn in brown

Small amounts of beige, brown, red, cream and gold coloured fingering (4-ply) yarn, and an oddment of gold lurex

Toy filling

Small brass bell

Two buttons and matching thread

Needles:

1 pair of 2.75mm (UK 12, US 2) and 1 pair of 4.5mm (UK 7, US 7) knitting needles

Sewing needle

Size:

Approx. 4in (10cm) tall

Instructions:

Body (make 2)

Using 4.5mm (UK 7, US 7) needles and chunky yarn, cast on 12 sts and work 2 rows in SS.

Next row: K1, M1, K to last st, M1, K1 (14 sts).

P 1 row.

Rep last 2 rows once more (16 sts).

Continue in SS for 10 rows.

Next row: K1, ssk, K to last 3 sts, K2tog, K1 (14 sts).

P 1 row.

Rep these 2 rows once more (12 sts).

Work 2 rows in SS.

Next row: K1, ssk, K to last 3 sts, K2tog, K1 (10 sts).

Next row: P4, cast off 2 sts, P to end of row (8 sts).

Turn and working on the first 4 sts, K1, ssk, K1 (3 sts).

P 1 row.

Next row: sl1, K2tog, psso. Fasten off rem st.

With RS facing, rejoin yarn to rem 4 sts, K1, K2tog, K1 (3 sts).

P 1 row.

Next row: sl1, K2tog, psso. Fasten off rem st.

Base

Using 4.5mm (UK 7, US 7) needles and chunky yarn, cast on 3 sts. Work 2 rows in SS.

Next row: K1, M1, K1, M1, K1 (5 sts).

P 1 row.

Rep the last 2 rows once more (7 sts).

Work 2 rows in SS.

Next row: K1, ssk, K1, K2tog, K1 (5 sts).

P 1 row.

Next row: K1, ssk, K2tog, K1 (3 sts).

P 1 row (3 sts).

Cast off rem sts.

Tummy

Using gold fingering (4-ply) yarn and 2.75mm (UK 12, US 2) knitting needles, cast on 10 sts, P 1 row.

Next row: K1, M1, K to last st, M1, K1 (12 sts).

P 1 row.

Rep the last 2 rows twice more (16 sts).

Work 4 rows in SS.

Next row: K6, ssk, K2tog, K6 (14 sts).

P 1 row.

Rep the last 2 rows, working one less st before and after decreases until 6 sts rem. Cast off rem sts.

Eyes

Cast on 4 sts using beige fingering (4-ply) yarn and 2.75mm (UK 12, US 2) knitting needles. P 1 row.

Next row: K1, M1, K2, M1, K1 (6 sts).

P 1 row.

Work in SS for 4 rows.

Next row: ssk, K2, K2tog (4 sts).

P 1 row. Cast off rem sts.

Beak

Cast on 5 sts using gold lurex yarn and 2.75mm (UK 12, US 2) needles and work 2 rows in SS.

Next row: K2tog, K1, K2tog. P 1 row.

Thread yarn through rem 3 sts and sew up seam of beak.

Wings

Cast on 3 sts using brown fingering (4-ply) yarn and 2.75mm (UK 12, US 2) knitting needles.

The wings are worked in GS throughout.

K 2 rows.

Next row: K1, M1, K to end of row (4 sts).

K 1 row.

Rep the last 2 rows until you have 8 sts.

Knit 12 rows.

Next row: K1, K2tog, K to last 3 sts, K2tog, K1.

K 1 row.

Rep the last 2 rows until 4 sts rem.

Next row: K2tog twice, cast off rem st and fasten off yarn.

Hat

Using 2.75mm (UK 12, US 2) needles and cream fingering (4-ply), cast on 22 sts and work 12 rows in GS.

Change to red fingering (4-ply) yarn.

Work 8 rows in SS.

Next row: (K1, K2tog) seven times, K1 (15 sts).

P 1 row.

Next row: (K1, K2tog) to end of row (10 sts).

P 1 row.

Work 2 rows in SS.

Next row: K2tog to end of row (5 sts).

P 1 row.

Thread yarn through rem sts, sew up side seam of hat, pulling the yarn slightly as you sew so the top of the hat folds over slightly. Fold GS edging up.

Making up

Sew up the side seams and stuff the owl with toy filling. Sew in the base, adding a piece of card to strengthen it if required. Attach the tummy, beak, wings and knitted eyes. Using a sewing needle and matching thread, sew on buttons for eyes. Attach the bell to the top of the hat.

Place on a mantelpiece or dressing table, or arrange several in a glass bowl. To create an alternative lily, use a pure wool light worsted (DK/8-ply) yarn in a deep pink-violet shade for the main part of the flower.

ARUM LILY

Instructions:

With white yarn and size 3mm (UK 11, US 2) DPN, cast on 8 sts and distribute between four needles.

Knit 3 rounds.

Round 4: inc in each st (16 sts).

Knit 3 rounds.

Round 8: (inc 1, k3) four times (20 sts).

Knit 2 rounds.

Round 11: (inc 1, k4) four times (24 sts).

Knit 2 rounds.

Round 14: inc 1, k5) four times (28 sts).

Knit 2 rounds.

Round 17: (inc 1, k6) four times (32 sts).

Knit 8 rounds.

Round 26: (inc 1, k7) four times (36 sts).

Round 27: (inc 1, k8) four times (40 sts).

Round 28: (inc 1, k9) four times (44 sts).

Round 29: (inc 1, k10) four times (48 sts).

Round 30: (inc 1, k11) four times (52 sts).

Round 31: (inc 1, k12) four times (56 sts).

Round 32: (inc 1, k13) four times (60 sts).

Purl 1 round.

Cast off knitwise.

Spadix

With orange yarn and size 3mm (UK 11, US 2) needles, cast on 20 sts.

Row 1: k all sts tbl.

Row 2: k16, turn.

Row 3: sl 1, k to end.

Row 4: k12, turn.

Row 5: sl 1, k to end.

Row 6: k to end.

Knit 6 rows.

Cast off.

Stem

With green yarn and two size 3mm (UK 11, US 2) DPN, cast on 5 sts.

Row 1: k5; do not turn but slide sts to other end of needle.

Rep this row until work measures 6.5cm (2½in); fasten off.

Making up

Stitch the cast-on and cast-off edges of the spadix together to form a tube. Stitch the base to the top of the stem. Insert into the flower and secure at the flower base.

Materials:

1 x ball each of light worsted (DK/8-ply) yarn in cream and pale blue, plus oddments in deep turquoise and green; 50g/137yd/125m

Toy stuffing

2 x 6mm round black beads for eyes

Black embroidery thread or floss for features

19¾in (50cm) of narrow velvet ribbon in deep turquoise

2 x small sparkly, flower-shaped buttons

Tiny bunch of paper or silk flowers

Tools:

1 pair 3.25mm (UK 10, US 3) knitting needles

Sewing needles

Stitch holder

ELLIE BOUQUET BEAR

Instructions:

Make the bear in cream yarn following the instructions on page 41.

Dress (bodice front)

Using pale blue yarn, cast on 24 sts.

Rows 1–6: SS.

Rows 7–8: cast off 2 sts at beg of each row.

Rows 9–10: SS.

Row 11: dec 1 st at each end of row (18 sts).

Row 12: purl.

Rows 13–16: SS.

Divide for neck

Work 7 sts, slip next 4 sts on to stitch holder, work 7 sts.

Continue on first 7 sts for side of neck.

Dec 1 st at neck edge on next and following alt rows until 4 sts rem.

Cast off.

Work other side to match.

Bodice back

Work rows 1–16 of bodice front.

Rows 17–21: SS.

Cast off.

Skirt

With RS facing, pick up and knit 24 sts along cast-on edge of bodice front.

Next row: purl.

Next row: knit twice into each st (48 sts).

Continue in SS until skirt measures 4cm (1½in). Change to deep turquoise and work a further 4 rows SS, followed by 3 rows GS.

Cast off.

Repeat the above on bodice back.

Neckband

Join one shoulder seam.

With RS facing, pick up and knit 5 sts down one side of neck, 4 sts from stitch holder across front of neck, 5 sts up other side of neck and 10 sts around back of neck (rem 4 sts will form other shoulder).

Next row: knit.

Cast off knitwise.

Sleeve frills (make 2)

Using pale blue, cast on 24 sts loosely.

Row 1: purl.

Row 2: knit, inc 12 sts evenly across row (36 sts).

Rows 3–4: SS.

Row 5: change to deep turquoise and knit 1 row.

Cast off.

Shoes (make 2)

Using turquoise yarn, cast on 14 sts.

Next row: knit.

Next row: inc in each st across row (28 sts).

Work 5 rows GS.

Next row: K2tog, K8, (K2tog) four times, K8, K2tog.

Next row: K9, (K2tog) twice, K9.

Next row: knit.

Cast off. Stitch the seam along the base and back of the shoe. Put a tiny amount of stuffing inside the shoe, place the base of the leg inside the shoe and stitch it in place. Sew a sparkly button on the front of each one.

Making up

Stitch one shoulder seam and work the neckband in deep turquoise. Sew the side seams, and turn right-side out. Slip the dress on to the bear. Catch together the neckband and shoulder seam neatly. Sew the sleeve frill ends together then stitch them to the armholes, easing to fit if needed. Tie a length of ribbon around the waist and finish with a bow at the back of the dress. Wrap some green yarn tightly around the base of the flowers, and secure. Catch the bear's paws to each side of the flowers to hold them in place. Tie a small bow from some ribbon and sew it to the top of the bear's head.

WISE OWL PHONE SOCK

Materials:
1 ball of light worsted (DK/8-ply) yarn in beige, and an oddment in dark brown; 50g/137yd/125m

Small pieces of cream and brown felt

Toy stuffing

2 black buttons

Snap fastener

Needles:
1 pair of 4mm (UK 8, US 6) knitting needles

Embroidery needle and brown sewing thread

Scissors

Tape measure

Knitting note
Buttonhole stitch is similar to blanket stitch (although not the same) – it catches a loop of the thread on the surface of your work, then the needle is pushed back through the piece at a right angle. The stitch should look like an 'L'. Always keep even spaces between stitches.

Instructions:
Cast on 32 sts in beige using the finger or thumb method (see page 18).

Row 1: Slip first stitch then purl to end.

Row 2: knit.

Next rows: Work in st st, starting with a purl row, until work measures 1½in (4cm).

Next row: With right side facing, k6, join in dark brown yarn, k4 (twist yarns loosely across back to prevent holes), knit to end in beige yarn.

Next rows: Continue with this colour pattern in st st until work measures 4in (10cm).

Cast off 16 sts.

Next rows: Work st st on the remaining sts until work measures 6¼in (16cm) from cast-on edge.

Cast off loosely.

Making up
Join the seams using mattress stitch. Attach a press stud (snap fastener) using a needle and thread, then cut out a triangle from the dark brown felt for the beak. Attach it using the needle and thread.

Make an eye by cutting out a pair of 1in (2.5cm) cream felt circles and filling them with toy stuffing. Place the eye on the owl's face and stitch it in place using buttonhole stitch and brown thread. Place a button in the centre of the eye and stitch it on. Add a second eye in the same way.

Cut several 3⅛in (8cm) lengths of yarn and tie them into the sides of the owl's head as ear tufts to finish.

These delightful mug hugs will bring a touch of summer sunshine to your tea or coffee break. In the second design, the long edges are knitted using green only, with three bold sunflower buttons attached.

STRAWBERRY FAIR MUG HUG

Materials:

1 ball each of fingering (4-ply) yarn in bright red and green, plus an oddment in pale yellow; 50g/191yd/175m

3 x strawberry buttons

Green flower button

Needles:

1 pair 3.25mm (UK 10, US 3) knitting needles

Size:

9½ x 2¾in (24 x 7cm)

Instructions:

Using green yarn, cast on 53 sts.

Work in GS.

Knit 2 rows.

Change to yellow yarn and knit 2 rows.

Break yellow yarn and knit 2 rows in green.

Change to red yarn and work pattern, joining in and breaking off yellow yarn as needed. Strand yarn across the back of the work.

Rows 1–4: beg with RS facing, work in SS.

Row 5: K2 red, 1 yellow, (3 red, 1 yellow) to last 2 sts, K2 red.

Rows 6–8: continue in SS using red.

Row 9: K4 red, 1 yellow, (3 red, 1 yellow) to last 4 sts, K4 red.

Rows 10–12: as rows 6–8.

Row 13: as row 5.

Rows 14–16: as rows 6–8.

Break off red and yellow and change to green. Work 2 rows in GS.

Join in yellow and work 2 rows in GS.

Break yellow and knit 2 rows green. Cast off.

Button edge

With RS facing and using green yarn, pick up and knit 21 sts evenly along one short edge.

Continue in GS.

Dec 1 st at each end of next and every alt row until 9 sts rem. Cast off.

Buttonhole edge

Work as button edge until 15 sts rem.

Next row: to make buttonhole, K2tog, K5, yrn twice, K2tog, K to last 2 sts, K2tog.

Next row: knit, dropping the yrn of the previous row and knitting into the loops.

Dec as before until 9 sts rem. Cast off.

Making up

Work in all ends neatly. Sew the strawberry buttons in place and stitch on the flower button to correspond with the buttonhole.

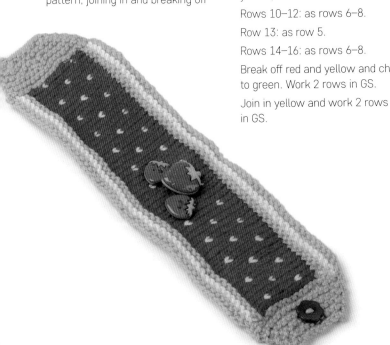

ICED DOUGHNUT

Materials:

1 ball each of fingering (4-ply) yarn in beige and pink; 50g/191yd/175m

Pink seed beads

Pink bugle beads

Toy stuffing

Needles:

Set of 4 x 3.25mm (UK 10, US 3) DPN

Instructions:

Cast on 30 sts using beige yarn – 10 sts on each of 3 needles.

Rounds 1–6: knit.

Round 7: knit, increasing 2 sts randomly on each needle (12 sts on each needle; 36 sts in total).

Rounds 8–10: continue, increasing 2 sts randomly on each needle until there are 18 sts on each (54 sts in total).

Rounds 11–18: knit.

Rounds 19–26: break yarn and change to pink. Knit 8 rounds.

Rounds 27–30: dec 2 sts randomly on each needle until 10 sts on each needle (30 sts in total).

Rounds 31–36: knit.

Cast off.

Making up
Stretch the stitching round into a doughnut shape and fill with toy stuffing. Using matching wool sew the doughnut together. Decorate with seed and bugle beads.

The white-iced doughnut is knitted using cream and beige fingering (4-ply) yarn and decorated with seed and bugle beads in pastel shades.

What's Up, Doc?
For a smaller carrot, cast on 6 sts, knit 1 round,
then inc1 in each st on 2nd round (12 sts). On
round 3, (k1, inc1) six times (18 sts), knit 12
rounds, then continue as for the large carrot,
from ** (round 53 onwards).

CARROT

Materials:

1 ball of light worsted (DK/8-ply) cotton or linen yarn in orange; 50g/109yd/100m

1 ball of light worsted (DK/8-ply) bamboo blend yarn in light green; 50g/104yd/95m

Toy stuffing

Needles:

Set of four 3mm (UK 11, US 2) DPN and 1 pair of 3mm (UK 11, US 2) knitting needles

Size:

Approx. 6¾in (17cm) long excluding the stalk, and 1¾in (4.25cm) in diameter at the widest point

Instructions:

Carrot

With 3mm (UK 11, US 2) DPN and orange yarn, cast on 9 sts and divide between three needles.

Round 1: k.

Round 2: inc in each st (18 sts).

Round 3: (k1, inc 1) nine times (27 sts).

Rounds 4–23: k.

Round 24: (k7, k2tog) three times (24 sts).

Rounds 25–33: k.

Round 34: (k6, k2tog) three times (21 sts).

Rounds 35–44: k.

Round 45: (k5, k2tog) three times (18 sts).

Rounds 46–52: k.

**Round 53: (k4, k2tog) three times (15 sts).

Rounds 54–57: k.

Round 58: (k3, k2tog) three times (12 sts).

Rounds 59–61: k.

Round 62: (k2, k2tog) three times (9 sts).

Rounds 63–64: k.

Round 65: (k1, k2tog) three times (6 sts).

Rounds 66–67: k.

Cut yarn and thread through rem sts.

Fronds

With 3mm (UK 11, US 2) knitting needles and light green yarn, cast on 15 sts using cable method.

Row 1: k.

Row 2: cast off 11 sts, k to end (4 sts).

Row 3: k4, turn and cast on 11 sts using cable method (15 sts).

Rows 4–11: Rep rows 2 and 3.

Cast off all sts.

Making up

Fill the carrot with toy stuffing; for a knobbly carrot, do not stuff too firmly, or use recycled fabric scraps such as old tights instead. Roll up the fronds and stitch in place.

Plum Crazy
Plums are very versatile, and can be eaten as they are or made into jam, puddings, wine or even brandy – while this knitted version makes a permanent fruity decoration or gift.

PLUM

Materials:

1 ball of fingering (4-ply) wool or wool blend yarn in violet; 50g/191yd/175m

Small amount of light worsted (DK/8-ply) yarn in brown; 50g/137yd/125m

Toy stuffing

Tools:

1 pair of 2.25mm (UK 13, US 1) knitting needles and 1 pair of 3mm (UK 11, US 2) DPN

Instructions:

Plum

With 2.25mm (UK 13, US 1) needles and violet yarn, cast on 6 sts.

Row 1: inc1 in each st to end (12 sts).

Row 2: p.

Row 3: k.

Row 4: p.

Row 5: inc1 in each st to end (24 sts).

Rows 6–8: as rows 2–4.

Row 9: (k1, inc1) twelve times (36 sts).

Rows 10–26: Beg with a p row, work in st st (1 row purl, 1 row knit).

Row 27: (k1, k2tog) twelve times (24 sts).

Rows 28–30: as rows 2–4.

Row 31: (k2tog) twelve times (12 sts).

Rows 32–34: as rows 2–4.

Row 35: (k2tog) six times.

Cut yarn, leaving a tail, and thread through rem 6 sts.

Stalk

With two 3mm (UK 11, US 2) DPN and brown yarn, cast on 2 sts.

Row 1: k2; do not turn but slide sts to other end of needle.

Rep row 1 until stalk measures ¾in (2cm); cast off.

Making up

With the right sides together, stitch the seam in backstitch, leaving a small opening. Turn the right sides out, stuff firmly and close the seam, pulling it up slightly. Next, take the needle through the plum from the top (cast-on edge) to the bottom. Pull the yarn gently to create a dimple in the top, then fasten off. Attach the stem by threading the yarn end into a needle and passing the needle down through the plum from top to bottom. The finished plum is approximately 2⅜in (6cm) tall (excluding the stalk) and 2¼in (5.5cm) in diameter.

These pretty little gloves will keep your hands warm on a winter's day. I have chosen muted greys for the stripes, but they would be equally pretty in bright or subtle colours.

Knitting note

m1: knit the loop between two sts.

Materials:

1 ball each of light worsted (DK/8-ply) merino yarn in light grey (A) and dark grey (B); 100g/273yd/250m

2 small, striped buttons

Needles:

1 pair of 4mm (UK 8, US 6) knitting needles

CHIC STRIPEY CUFFS

Instructions:

Right hand

Using 4mm (UK 8, US 6) needles and yarn A, cast on 40 sts, then ktbl to form a neat edge.

Rows 1–2: *k2, p2*, rep from * to * to end of row.

Change to yarn B. From this point on, change colours every two rows to form the stripes.

Rows 3–14: st st.

Shape for thumb

Row 15: k20, m1, k5, m1, k15 (42 sts).

Rows 16–18: st st, starting with a purl row.

Row 19: k20, m1, k7, m1, k15 (44 sts).

Rows 20–22: st st, starting with a purl row.

Row 23: k20, m1, k9, m1, k15 (46 sts).

Rows 24–26: st st, starting with a purl row.

Row 27: k20, m1, k11, m1, k15 (48 sts).

Rows 28–30: st st, starting with a purl row.

Divide for thumb

Row 31: (RS) k33, turn.

Row 32: p13.

Rows 33–38: Working on these 13 sts only, knit in st st, continuing in the stripe sequence.

Row 39: *k2, p2*, rep from * to * to last st, k1.

Row 40: p1, *k2, p2*, rep from * to * to end of row.

Cast off all sts.

Using a tapestry needle and mattress stitch, sew the side seam of the thumb. With RS facing, rejoin yarn and pick up and knit 2 sts from the base of the thumb, then knit to end of row (37 sts).

Next row: Purl.

Next 15 rows: st st.

Next row: *k2, p2*, rep from * to * to last st, k1.

Next row: p1, *k2, p2*, rep from * to * to end of row. Cut off yarn B.

Cast off all sts following rib pattern.

Left hand

Work as for right hand up to the shaping of the thumb.

Row 15: k15, m1, k5, m1, k20 (42 sts).

Rows 16–30: Work increases as for right hand using the spacing of row 15 above – start increase rows with k15 sts and end with k20 sts.

Divide for thumb

Next row: (RS) k28, turn.

Next row: p13.

Next 8 rows: As for right-hand thumb.

Cast off and join the side seam of the thumb. With RS facing, rejoin yarn and pick up and knit 2 sts from base of thumb, then knit to end of row.

Next row: Purl.

Next 15 rows: st st.

Next row: *k2, p2*, rep from * to * to last st, k1.

Next row: p1, *k2, p2*, rep from * to * to end of row. Cut off yarn B.

Cast off all sts following rib pattern.

Bow (make 4)

Cast on 13 sts using 4mm (UK 8/US 6) needles and yarn A, then ktbl to form a neat edge.

Rows 1–2: st st.

Cast off all sts. Weave in all loose ends.

Making up

With RS facing, use a tapestry needle and mattress stitch to sew up the side seams. Match the stripes as you sew up your gloves. Weave in all loose ends.

Place bows on the front of the glove, three light grey stripes down from the finger end. Cross the strips in the centre and place a small, striped button in the middle. Sew the button in place using yarn B (this will also secure the bow onto the glove).

CLASSIC BEANIE

Materials:

2 balls of worsted (aran/10-ply) pure wool tweed
yarn in russet; 50g/105yd/96m

Needles:

1 pair of 4mm (UK 8, US 6) and 1 pair of 5mm (UK 6,
US 8) knitting needles

Size:

To fit an average adult male head

Instructions:

With 4mm (UK 8, US 6) needles cast on 92 sts.
Row 1: (k2, p2) to end.
Rep row 1 fifteen times more.
Change to 5mm (UK 6, US 8) needles and, beg with a k row, work 24 rows in stocking stitch.
Row 51: (k13, k2tog) six times, k2 (86 sts).
Row 52 and each even-numbered (WS) row: purl.
Row 53: (k12, k2tog) six times, k2 (80 sts).
Row 55: (k11, k2tog) six times, k2 (74 sts).
Row 57: (k10, k2tog) six times, k2 (68 sts).
Row 59: (k9, k2tog) six times, k2 (62 sts).
Row 61: (k8, k2tog) six times, k2 (56 sts).
Row 63: (k7, k2tog) six times, k2 (50 sts).
Row 65: (k6, k2tog) six times, k2 (44 sts).
Row 67: (k5, k2tog) six times, k2 (38 sts).
Row 69: (k4, k2tog) six times, k2 (32 sts).
Row 71: (k3, k2tog) six times, k2 (26 sts).
Row 73: (k2, k2tog) six times, k2 (20 sts)
Row 74: (p2tog) ten times (10 sts).
Row 75: (k2tog) five times.
Cut yarn, leaving a tail, and thread through rem 5 sts.

Making up
Stitch up the back seam, reversing the seam on the ribbed band. Weave in any loose ends.

Mini Classic
For a child-size hat, follow the same pattern as for the adult hat but use light worsted (DK/8-ply) yarn; you should need only one 50g ball. Cast on using 3.25mm (UK 10, US 3) needles and work 16 rows in rib, then change to 4mm (UK 8, US 6) needles before continuing. Check your gauge (tension): you should have 19 sts and 29 rows to 4in (10cm) using 4mm needles.

Harvest Feast

This simple, elegant cosy makes a gorgeous table decoration ideal for Thanksgiving celebrations or Hallowe'en parties.

Materials:

1 ball of worsted (aran/10-ply) yarn in orange, plus oddments in brown and green; 50g/93yd/85m

Tools:

1 pair of 4mm (UK 8, US 6) knitting needles and 1 pair of 4mm (UK 8, US 6) DPN

2 stitch holders

Gauge (tension)

5 sts = 1in (2.5cm).

PUMPKIN TEA COSY

Instructions:

Make two.

Using orange yarn and 4mm (UK 8, US 6) needles, cast on 42 sts.

Knit in SS for 12 rows.

Row 13: k4, p1, *k7, p1* repeat from * to *, until last 5 sts then p1, k4.

Row 14: purl.

Repeat rows 13 and 14 until work measures 15cm (6in) from the cast-on edge.

Shape the top
Row 1: k7, k2tog, *k6, k2tog* rep from * to * to last st, k1.

Row 2: purl.

Row 3: k6, k2tog, *k5, k2tog*, rep from * to * to last st, k1.

Row 4: purl.

Row 5: k5, k2tog, *k4, k2tog*, rep from * to * to last st, k1.

Row 6: purl.

Row 7: k4, k2tog, *k3, k2tog*, rep from * to * to last st, k1.

Row 8: purl.

Row 9: k3, k2tog, *k2, k2tog*, rep from * to * to last st, k1.

Row 10: purl.

Row 11: k2, k2tog, *k1, k2tog*, rep from * to * to last st, k1.

Row 12: purl.

Row 13: k1, k2tog, *k2tog*, rep from * to * to last st, k1.

Row 14: purl.

Row 15: change to brown yarn and k1, k2tog, k1, k2tog, k1.

Row 16: purl.

Row 17: knit.

Row 18: purl.

Row 19: knit.

Cut yarn and place sts on stitch holder.

Making up
Place the wrong sides of the cosy together (right sides out). Thread a tapestry needle with the brown tail on the back stitch holder. Graft the sts on the stitch holders together.

Sew the stem
Continuing with the brown tail of yarn, sew down one side of the stem. Fasten off and hide tail in seam. Repeat on other side of stem.

Sew the top
Thread a tapestry needle with one of the orange tails at the top of the cosy. Sew down one side for 3in (7.5cm). Fasten off, hide tail in the seam. Repeat on other side of cosy.

Sew the bottom
Thread a tapestry needle with one of the orange tails of yarn from the cast on edge. Sew up one side for 1½in (4cm). Fasten off, hide tail in seam. Repeat on other side of cosy.

Leaf
Using green yarn and the 4mm (UK 8, US 6) DPN, cast on 4 sts.

Row 1: purl.

Row 2: k2, kfb, k1.

Row 3: purl.

Row 4: k2, kfb, k2.

Row 5: purl.

Row 6: knit.

Row 7: purl.

Row 8: k2, k2tog, k2.

Row 9: purl.

Row 10: k2, k2tog, k1.

Row 11: purl.

Row 12: k1, k2tog, k1.

Row 13: purl.

Row 14: sk2po.

Fasten off.

Stalk
Using green yarn and the 4mm (UK 8, US 6) DPN, cast on 2 sts.

Row 1: k2; do not turn but slide sts to other end of needle.

Repeat this until work measures approximately 2in (5cm).

Fasten off.

Using one of the tails, sew stalk to the top of the leaf.

Vine
Using green yarn and the 4mm (UK 8, US 6) DPN, cast on 20 sts.

Cast off the 20 sts.

Fasten off.

Twist the vine to help it 'curl'. Attach the leaf and vine. Position the stalk and vine on the base of the stem and sew in place. Weave in all loose ends.

Motif charts
Choose from snowflake, heart, Christmas tree or reindeer motifs for your bunting designs.

NORDIC BUNTING

Materials:

1 ball of fingering (4-ply) yarn in red, and a small
amount in cream; 50g/191yd/175m

Tools:

1 pair 3.25mm (UK 10, US 3) knitting needles

3mm crochet hook (optional)

Size:

Each pennant approx. 4¼ x 2¾in (11 x 7cm)

Instructions:

Using red yarn, cast on 1 st.

Next row: K into the front, back and front of the
stitch (3sts).

Next row: K1, P1, K1.

Next row: K1, M1, P1, M1, K1 (5 sts).

Next row: K1, P1, K1, P1, K1.

Next row: K1, P1, M1, K1, M1, P1, K1 (7 sts).

Next row (RS): K1, P1, K3, P1, K1.

Next row: (K1, P1) three times, K1.

Continue as follows:

Row 1: **K1, P1, K1,** M1, work to last 3 sts, M1, **K1, P1,
K1**.

Row 2: **K1, P1, K1**, work to last 3 sts, **K1, P1, K1**.

Keeping the 3 border sts in moss st (marked in bold),
work these 2 rows a further six times, inc either side of
the central SS panel until you have 21 sts.

Work 2 rows with no further shaping.

Keeping moss st edges, work 20 rows of your selected
chart (see opposite).

Work a further 2 rows.

Work 4 rows in moss st. Cast off all sts.

Making up

Either sew the corners of the pennants together or
crochet a chain stitch between the pennants and single
crochet (*UKdouble crochet*) across the top of each one
to join them together.

Use the white daisy to decorate a summer hat or beach bag. Use blue yarn to make a Michaelmas daisy, or create a customised daisy in your favourite colour.

DAISY

Materials:

1 ball of light worsted (DK/8-ply) cotton
  yarn in white; 50g/170yd/155m

Small amount of light worsted (DK/8-ply)
  acrylic bouclé yarn in yellow

Round button, 1¼in (3cm)

Needles:

1 pair of 2.25mm (UK 13, US 1) knitting needles

Size:

Approx. 6in (15cm) across

Instructions:

Petals (made in 1 piece)

With white cotton yarn and size 2.25mm (UK 13, US 1)
needles, cast on 14 sts.

Row 1: k all sts tbl.

Row 2: k11, turn.

Row 3: k to end.

Row 4: k.

Row 5: cast off 12, k rem st.

Row 6: k2, cast on 12.

Rep rows 1–6 fourteen times, omitting row 6 on final rep
and casting off last 2 sts instead.

Break yarn and fasten off.

Centre

With yellow bouclé yarn and size 2.25mm needles,
cast on 6 sts.

Row 1: k.

Row 2: inc 1, k to last st, inc 1 (8 sts).

Row 3: k.

Row 4: inc 1, k to last st, inc 1 (10 sts).

Row 5: k.

Row 6: inc 1, k to last st, inc 1 (12 sts).

Knit 8 rows.

Row 15: sl 1, k1, psso, k8, k2tog (10 sts).

Row 16: k.

Row 17: sl 1, k1, psso, k6, k2tog (8 sts).

Row 18: k.

Row 19: sl 1, k1, psso, k4, k2tog (6 sts).

Cast off.

Making up

Join the two ends of the petals to form a ring. Stitch
a gathering thread along the base of all the petals and
pull up tightly to gather. Stitch a running thread around
the edge of the centre piece, place the button inside and
pull up the yarn to gather; fasten off securely. Stitch the
covered button to the centre of the flower.

If you would like more information about knitting
techniques, try the following book by Search Press:

Knitting for the Absolute Beginner by
Alison Dupernex, Search Press, 2012

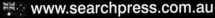